Quick Hors d'oeuvres

A ONE FOOT IN THE KITCHEN COOKBOOK

Written and Compiled by
CYNDI DUNCAN AND GEORGIE PATRICK

Illustrated by
COLETTE McLAUGHLIN PITCHER

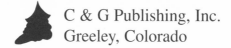 C & G Publishing, Inc.
Greeley, Colorado

Quick Hors d'oeuvres

Copyright © 2000
by Cyndi Duncan and Georgie Patrick

Library of Congress Control Number: 00-092532
ISBN 0-9700253-0-0
Printed in the United States of America

Illustrations by Colette McLaughlin Pitcher
Graphic Design by Gregory Effinger, for
Colorado Independent Graphics, Advertising and Reproduction, www.cigargraphics.com

Nutrition analysis has been calculated on Mastercook II software.

To the best of our knowledge, all information included in this book is correct and complete. The publisher and authors offer no guarantees and disclaim any liability attributed to its use.

Published by C & G Publishing, Inc.
P.O. Box 5199
Greeley, Colorado 80634-0103
For orders and information: (800) 925-3172

To the Georgies and the Cyndis of the world

who are too busy to get organized

who can't toss anything, even duplicate recipes

who believe their failure to remember anything is a conspiracy

who spend more on album supplies than on developing the pictures

who think being adventuresome means more than buying a different brand

and who aren't afraid to take chances

this book's for you!

Contents

Introduction

Now that we have completed *Quick Hors d'oeuvres,* fourth in the 'One Foot in the Kitchen' cookbook series, we find that we are still poles apart in our approach to cooking. In this new book, we have continued with our commitment to quick and easy recipes. But Cyndi is still cooking mostly from scratch and Georgie is getting better at being 'Queen of Easy'. Now she tells me she buys frozen meatballs, and and her guests are none the wiser when she adds one of her QUICK and easy sauces. Her kitchen shears are still getting a better workout than either of us are at the spa.

Georgie is right in thinking that the Cyndis of the world probably go to too much work, but doesn't it make us feel proud? Be reminded, too, that the Georgies are a bit smug about fooling their guests into thinking that their pantries and freezers are stockpiled with the fruits of their labors. I have learned though, as more and more time is enjoyed with friends, family and grand children, that any guilt from short-cut cooking is overcome by a lot of smugness when I can fool my guests by using Georgie's QUICK methods.

Entertaining is much more fun when the Cyndis and Georgies of the world can take a deep breath after preparing for a party, smile at their QUICK results and enjoy their guests to the max. More and more this Cyndi is leaning toward Georgie's time-saving approach to cooking knowing that delicious, time-saving creations are the inevitable outcome.

Meeting in the middle isn't such a bad thing, when I know I can reserve really in-depth cooking for that rare day when I have nothing else demanding my time.

Cyndi

Footnotes from Cyndi and Georgie

Entertaining is fun but too often we find ourselves rushing to wipe down the bathroom, clean the front door window and, most of all, finish the hors d'oeuvres, leaving little time for getting dressed and combing our hair. Quick Hors d'oeuvres was created to help eliminate the last minute hassle and let you enjoy your guests. Ultimately, we want you to be secure in the knowledge that the food is ready. Since we sometimes use different methods in our QUICK cooking, we want to share some helpful hints to make your kitchen user friendly.

Read recipes before preparing to make sure you have all of the ingredients and understand instructions.

Be aware that recipes will serve more guests than specified if you are offering a large selection of hors d'oeuvres.

Shop sales for staple and pantry items. Keep a variety of cheeses, crackers, meats and veggies on hand for unexpected guests.

Date spices and replace yearly to maintain freshness. Keep minced and chopped onion, green peppers, chives and cilantro in your pantry for use at times when you don't have fresh produce on hand.

Use plastic squeeze bottles to store marinades and sauces; then when you are ready to grill, squeeze on meat and spread with pastry brush. Discard any marinade in which meat has been marinated to avoid any contamination between meat and marinade.

Drop a whole, peeled potato in a hot mixture while cooking if it has been over salted. The potato will absorb the excess salt.

Freeze juices in ice cube trays or ice ring form to use in drinks or punches.

Microwave cream cheese 10-15 seconds to soften if cream cheese has not been left out to reach room temperature.

Use light mayonnaise, sour cream and cream cheese to reduce calories and fat grams.

Add life to a bunch of cilantro by removing from plastic bag, trimming the stems, and placing upright in jar of water. Wash just before using to lessen deterioration.

Notes:

Beverages

CRANBERRY PUNCH

Georgie's friend, Pat, first served this tangy punch at a gourmet group dinner. It has become a Patrick favorite.

1 16-ounce can jellied cranberry sauce
1/2 cup lemon juice
1 cup orange juice
1/2 teaspoon almond extract
Cracked ice, ice cubes or ice ring
1 pint ginger ale

In large mixing bowl, blend cranberry sauce, lemon juice, orange juice and almond extract. Pour over ice. Add ginger ale just before serving. Serves 10-12.

Per serving: 91 calories; 0.1 fat grams

 Make festive ice cubes by filling ice cube trays with juice and fruit. Use bundt pans or shaped muffin tins or cake pans for uniquely shaped ice rings.

GRAPE JUICE CRUSH

Our children loved this cold drink when they were young.

2 cups grape juice
1 cup orange juice
1/4 cup lemon juice
1/2 cup sugar
2 cups ice water
1 quart ginger ale, chilled

In large pitcher, mix fruit juices. Add sugar and stir until sugar is dissolved. Add ginger ale. Pour into glasses filled with cracked ice. Serves 12.

Per serving: 96 calories; 0.1 fat grams

 To make popsicles for children, pour into small kitchen cups, insert a popsicle stick when partially frozen, and freeze until firm.

CHRISTMAS PUNCH

After being served this at newcomers club, we served this punch at one of our cookie exchanges.

4 cups cranberry juice
2 cups orange juice
1 cup pineapple juice
3/4 cup lemon juice
1 cup sugar
1/2 teaspoon almond extract
2 cups ginger ale, chilled
1 pint pineapple sherbet

In punch bowl, blend juices, sugar and almond extract. Refrigerate. To serve, stir in ginger ale and sherbet. Serves 10-12.

Per serving: 200 calories; 0.5 fat grams

FALL NECTAR

This is a nice, refreshing drink on an Indian summer day.

4 cups apple cider
4 cups ginger ale
ice cubes
4 apple slices
Dash of cinnamon

Combine apple cider and ginger ale in a pitcher. Pour into glass over ice. Garnish with apple slices and dash of cinnamon. Serves 8.

Per serving: 137 calories; 0.4 fat grams

Make pretty apple rings by thinly slicing apple crosswise. Use small cookie cutter in desired shape to cut out seeds in the center. If prepared ahead, dip in lemon juice to prevent browning.

MULLED CIDER

The enticing aroma of this spicy drink fills your home as you greet your guests.

1/2 cup brown sugar
1 teaspoon whole allspice
1 teaspoon whole cloves
1/4 teaspoon salt
Dash or two nutmeg
1 3-inch cinnamon stick
2 quarts apple cider
1/2 orange, sliced, unpeeled

Tie allspice and cloves in a small piece of cheese-cloth or place them in a spice ball. In large saucepan or slow cooker, combine all ingredients. Slowly bring to a boil. Cover and simmer 20 minutes (if in slow cooker, heat on high for 1 hour then lower heat). Remove spices. Ladle into mug. Place orange slices on top. Serves 6-8.

Per serving: 160 calories; 0.4 fat grams

 To make attractive floating orange star slices, insert 5 whole cloves at equal intervals around outside peel of each orange slice. Cut out a wedge of peel and pulp between each 2 cloves to form star points.

COFFEE ROYAL

Those of us who like the lattés and cappuccinos will have to have this treat often. Cyndi has served this as a dessert at the end of a light meal.

2 quarts strong coffee, chilled
1 cup dark rum
1/2 cup sugar
2 quarts vanilla ice cream
2 cups frozen whipped topping

Combine coffee, rum and sugar in large punch bowl. Stir in ice cream and whipped topping, just enough to leave small bits unblended for garnish. Garnish with chocolate curls on a dollop of whipped cream, if desired. Serves 20-25.

Per serving: 135 calories; 5.4 fat grams

Foot Notes

To make chocolate curls, use a square of bakers chocolate at room temperature; with potato/carrot peeler, shave off curls. For a QUICK alternative substitute chopped chocolate candy bar or sprinkles for chocolate curls.

To make QUICK latté, refrigerate leftover coffee to chill. Fill glass with ice, coffee and flavored, non-dairy creamer.

Beverages

SMOOTHIES

Smoothies are nutritious drinks usually made by combining blended fruits and fruit juices that often include a creamy base of milk, ice cream or tangy yogurt.

Colorado Sunshine Smoothie

    1 6-ounce can frozen lemonade
    2 lemonade cans water
    6 strawberries, washed, stemmed
    1/4 medium cantaloupe, peeled and cut
       in chunks

Breakfast Delight Smoothie

    1 1/2 cups orange juice
    1/2 cup canned or fresh pineapple
       chunks
    1 frozen banana, cut into chunks
    1/4 cup orange yogurt
    3 ice cubes

Hot Tomato Smoothie

    2 cups tomato juice
    1/2 small jalapeno pepper, chopped
    2 slices onion, chopped
    2 pinches parsley
    2 teaspoons garlic powder

In all recipes, combine in blender and mix on high for one minute. Pour into glasses over ice, if desired, garnish and serve. Serves 4.

Per serving:
Colorado Sunshine, 146 calories; 0.9 fat grams
Breakfast Delight, 94 calories; 0.7 fat grams
Hot Tomato, 55 calories; 0.2 fat grams

Foot Notes

Using frozen fruits will produce thicker smoothies. Frozen bananas give the same creamy texture as ice cream or yogurt.

To keep smoothies cold without diluting freeze fruit cubes, fruit juices or leftover smoothies to use in place of ice.

Create your own perfect smoothies using the following formula: to 1/2-1 cup liquid and 1 cup fruit or vegetables add desired flavorings, cereal, nuts, seeds, herbs and supplements.

MIXES FOR HOT DRINKS

We usually have a steady flow of family and friends visiting our homes, and like the convenience of having these beverages on hand. Mixes can be stored in jars or decorative canisters.

Hot Cocoa

    3 cups instant non-dairy creamer
    3 cups instant dry milk
    1 1/3 cups sugar
    1 cup cocoa
Put 4-6 tablespoons mix in mug of hot water

Spiced Tea

    1 3-ounce package lemonade mix
    1 1/2 cups sugar
    1 cup instant tea
    1 1/2 cups orange-flavored drink mix
    2 teaspoons cinnamon
    1 teaspoon cloves
Put 2-3 tablespoons mix in mug of hot water

Swiss Mocha

    1 cup instant coffee (fine grind)
    2 cups instant non-dairy creamer
    2 cups hot cocoa mix
    1 cup powdered sugar
    1 tablespoon cocoa
    1 cup instant dry milk
Put 2-3 tablespoons mix in mug of hot water

For each recipe, combine all ingredients in large bowl. Store in airtight container up to six months. Makes 1-2 quarts of mix.

Per serving:
Hot Cocoa, 82 calories; 0.4 fat grams
Spiced Tea, 93 calories; 0 fat grams
Swiss Mocha, 77 calories; 0.5 fat grams

 Foot Note For large groups mix together enough mix and hot water to fill a teapot. Chill the Swiss Mocha drink and serve in a punch bowl.

HOT BUTTERED RUM

Relax on a cold, wintery night with a mug of this drink and read a good book or take a quiet snooze. Its spicy aroma is soothing and the taste superb.

2 pounds brown sugar
1 cup butter, softened
1/2 teaspoon nutmeg
1/2 teaspoon cinnamon
1/2 teaspoon cloves
Rum
Cinnamon sticks

In large bowl, cream together brown sugar, butter and spices. Store in airtight container in refrigerator indefinitely. To serve, stir 3 tablespoons of mixture and 1 jigger of rum into mug of boiling water. Use a cinnamon stick to stir. Garnish with whipped topping if desired. Serves 20.

Per serving: 348 calories; 9.1 fat grams

 This mixture should stay soft, but in case it should get dry, lay an apple slice on top of mixture and seal. The apple will keep it moist.

SPARKLING ORANGE EGGNOG

The orange flavoring is a very refreshing addition to this traditional drink.

2 quarts orange juice
1/2 cup lemon juice
2 quarts eggnog
1 quart vanilla ice cream
1 quart chilled ginger ale
Nutmeg, optional

In a large punch bowl, combine juices and eggnog. Keep chilled until ready to serve. At last minute, spoon ice cream on top of mixture. Slowly pour ginger ale along edges. This will cause a frothy surface for the punch. Give one gentle stir with ladle. Serves 30.

Per serving: 147 calories; 4.3 fat grams

 If desired, garnish with the orange stars that are mentioned on page 4,

SNEAKY PETES

Make this ahead to serve on hot summer days. Georgie has pleased guests with this delicious drink since receiving the recipe from her friend, Sally.

1 12-ounce can frozen lemonade, thawed
1 12-ounce can frozen limeade, thawed
1 1/2 quarts cranapple juice
1 cup vodka
1 cup water
Sweet and sour mix

In large container, combine all ingredients except the sour mix. Freeze. To serve, use ice cream scoop to spoon 1/2 cup of mixture into short glass. Pour sweet and sour mix over mixture until glass is full. Serves 20.

Per serving: 132 calories; 0.1 fat grams

 The vodka keeps this mixture slushy so it is easy to scoop. Do not omit.

L.G.'S ANY DAY GROG

Most Navy men have a favorite drink; this creation is from Cyndi's husband. The family has enjoyed this one on every holiday for years.

1 quart orange juice
1 cup grapefruit juice
1/4 cup lemon juice
1/3 cup frozen margarita mix
1 cup tequila
3-4 tablespoons salt
1 lime, cut in wedges

In large pitcher, combine all ingredients except lime and salt. With a piece of lime, moisten rim of short glass. Pour salt into flat dish and dip glasses. (L.G. sometimes sprinkles a pinch of salt on each drink instead of dipping the glass in salt). Fill glass and garnish with wedge of lime. Serves 8.

Per serving: 89 calories; 0.3fat grams

This drink can be blended with ice to make a delicious frozen drink. Serve in frosty glasses on those hot, sweltering days.

For Margarita Punch, substitute 4 cups pineapple juice and 2 large bottles of club soda for orange and grapefruit juices.

HOLIDAY PUNCH

It couldn't be easier and is beautiful on any table no matter what the occasion. This is Georgie's favorite open house punch.

1 10-ounce package frozen strawberries
1 bottle Rosé wine
1 6-ounce can limeade
2 bottles Cold Duck
Ice Ring

In punch bowl, mix strawberries, wine and limeade together. Let stand 1 hour at room temperature. Add Cold Duck and ice ring when ready to serve. Ladle into glass. Serves 25.

Per serving: 93 calories; 0 fat grams

 For decorative ice cubes, place half a strawberry in each ice tray section and fill with water. Freeze and add to punch.

SPICY WINE MIX

Keep this mix handy for A QUICK and easy way to spice up your favorite wine.

6 cups sugar
2 tablespoons cinnamon
2 tablespoons ground cloves
1 tablespoon allspice
3/4 teaspoon nutmeg
Dry red wine

Combine all ingredients; mix well. Store in an airtight container. To prepare hot spiced wine: In large mug, add 2 teaspoons dry mix to 1/2 cup hot water and microwave on high 30 seconds. Add 1 cup dry red wine and microwave 30 seconds. Do not boil. Serve with a cinnamon stick. Makes 6 1/4 cups mix.

Per serving: 179 calories; 0.0 fat grams

ICED TEA PUNCH

This punch can be served hot or cold.

1/2 cup water
1 cup sugar
1 1/3 cups lemon juice
1 1/2 cups brewed tea
1 8-ounce jar maraschino cherries
    and syrup

In large pan, boil sugar and water 5 minutes. Combine with remaining ingredients. Serve hot, or cool and pour over crushed ice and serve cold, Serves 12.

Per serving: 104 calories; 0.0 fat grams

 Add a jigger of amaretto for a great drink.

FRUIT SHAKE

A good diet drink if using low fat ingredients. Not a sweet drink so a little sugar or an artificial sweetener may be used.

1/2 cup cottage cheese
1 cup milk
1 serving fruit (banana, orange, fresh or
    frozen berries)
Dash vanilla

Combine all ingredients in blender. Add ice cubes to chill or thicken. Serves 1.

Per serving: 291 calories; 7.2 fat grams

Almond extract and a fresh peach are excellent in this shake. Use sugar or honey to sweeten.

CREEPERS

Appropriately named because this drink is so smooth that it may creep up on you unexpectedly.

1 6-ounce can frozen limeade
1 limeade can light rum
1/4 cup liquid coffee creamer
Crushed ice

Combine all ingredients in blender. Blend 2-3 minutes until foamy. Pour into glasses over crushed ice. Serves 6.

Per serving: 138 calories; 2.0 fat grams

 Substitute vodka for the rum, omit coffee creamer and blend with 12 ice cubes for another great drink.

STRAWBERRY PUNCH

1 10-ounce package frozen strawberries, slightly thawed, or 1 1/2 cups fresh strawberries
3 6-ounce cans frozen lemonade concentrate
3 cans water
1/2 cup sugar
4 cups chilled ginger ale

Place strawberries in blender. Add lemonade, water and sugar. Cover and blend. Pour into punch bowl or pitcher. Add ginger ale. Serves 10.

Per serving: 186 calories; 0.1 fat grams

Add a juice can of rum to make Strawberry Daiquiris.

Notes:

Snacks

SPICED NUTS

Package these nuts in small plastic bags and put into decorative tins. Take along as a hostess gift or use in a gift basket. You can also freeze them to have on hand for last minute snacks.

1 egg white
1 tablespoon cold water
1 1/3 cups walnut halves
1 1/3 cups pecan halves
1 1/3 cups almonds
1/2 cup sugar
1-1 1/2 teaspoons apple pie spice

Preheat oven to 250°. In small bowl, beat egg white and water until frothy. Stir nuts into mixture to coat. Mix sugar and spice in bowl. Sprinkle over and toss to coat. Spread on buttered baking sheet; bake 45 minutes, stirring every 15 minutes. Remove and stir to separate. Cool. Store in airtight container. Makes 2 cups. Serves 12-16.

Per serving: 131 calories; 9.7 fat grams

Make **Orange Pecans** with 1/2 cup sugar, 1 tablespoon grated orange peel, 1/4 cup orange juice and 2 cups pecan halves. Bring sugar, orange peel and juice to rolling boil. Add pecans, stirring constantly until syrup is absorbed. Stir to separate. Turn onto baking sheet to cool.

CURRIED PECANS

These tasty little pecans are especially good served with cheese, crackers and fruit. Of course, pecans happen to be Georgie's very favorite nut, so she likes them any way she can get them.

2 tablespoons oil
1/4 teaspoon garlic powder
1/2 teaspoon salt
2 cups pecan halves
1/4-1/2 teaspoon curry powder

In heavy fry pan, combine oil, garlic powder and salt. Add nuts. Toast 7-10 minutes stirring constantly. Sprinkle curry on top and mix well. Cool. Store in air tight container. Serves 6-8.

Per serving: 126 calories; 13.1 fat grams

Can be 'baked' in microwave on microwave-safe plate. Bake on high for 1 1/2 minutes or until mixture is bubbly. Stir. Microwave another 12 minutes. Remove and stir to separate.

GORP

Cyndi and Georgie both take gorp on road trips and camping, but the Duncan family calls it 'birdseed'. It's never the same but always good.

1 16-ounce package plain candy-coated
   chocolate candies
1 16-ounce package peanut candy-coated
   chocolate candies
1 16-ounce jar dry-roasted peanuts
1 10-ounce can mixed nuts, optional
1 2-ounce package sunflower seed kernels
1 cup raisins

In large bowl, mix all ingredients together. Store for up to two weeks (if it lasts that long). Serves 20.

Per serving: 483 calories; 35.4 fat grams

If taking on a road trip, serve it in small paper kitchen cups so hands don't get messy. To keep chocolate from melting, store in air tight container in cooler.

You can substitute dried bananas, cranberries, cherries or apricots in place of or in addition to the raisins. Also, pretzels, small snack crackers, granola or popcorn can be added to the mixture.

OYSTER CRACKER SNACK

Keep some of these around to serve as 'croutons' on salads or soups.

1/2 cup oil
1 package dry ranch dressing mix
1 teaspoon dill weed
3/4 teaspoon garlic salt (garlic powder may
    be added for more flavor)
1/2 teaspoon lemon pepper
1 12-ounce package oyster crackers

Preheat oven to 300°. Place oyster crackers in large bowl; set aside. In small bowl, combine oil and dressing mix. Add dill weed, garlic salt and lemon pepper; mix well. Pour over crackers; stir to coat. Spread mixture on baking sheet. Bake 15 minutes. Pour onto paper toweling to cool. Store in airtight container up to two weeks. Serves 12.

Per serving: 301 calories; 22.6 fat grams

 When baking large amounts of these cracker/cereal mixes, use broiler pan or roaster; they are deeper and bigger than some baking sheets.

PARTY MIX

We almost didn't include this recipe knowing that everyone probably makes it. It is just too good to omit.

1 cup butter or margarine
6 teaspoons Worcestershire sauce
2 teaspoons seasoned salt
2 cups each wheat, corn and rice
    cereal squares
2 cups toasted oat cereal
3/4 cup salted dry roasted peanuts (or
    mixed nuts)
1 cup small pretzels, any shape
1 cup small fish or cheddar crackers

Preheat oven to 250°. Melt 1/2 cup butter in each of 2 large baking sheets in oven. Stir 3 teaspoons Worcestershire sauce and 1 teaspoon salt into butter in each baking sheet. Mix well. In very large bowl, mix together remaining ingredients. Spread half of cereal mix onto each baking sheet and stir to coat with butter mixture. Return to oven and bake 45 minutes, stirring every 15 minutes. Spread and cool on paper toweling. Serves 10-12.

Per serving: 467 calories; 25.3 fat grams

 Freeze in freezer bags and always have some on hand.

PRETZEL SNACK

QUICK and easy with a great combination of sweet and salty taste. Cyndi used to make small pretzel balls for school parties, placing them in small plastic bags and tying with appropriate colored ribbon.

1 1/2 cups pretzel sticks, broken in half
2 cups corn cereal squares
1 1/2 cups candy-coated chocolate pieces
1/2 cup butter
1/2 cup peanut butter
5 cups miniature marshmallows

In large bowl, gently toss pretzels, cereal and chocolate pieces. In large microwavable dish, melt butter, peanut butter and marshmallows, using high power for 1 minute intervals until melted. Pour over pretzel mix. Butter hands and shape into 1 1/2 to 2-inch balls. Serves 36.

Per serving: 154 calories; 6.9 fat grams

Foot Notes

Candy pieces now come in a variety of holiday colors. Add a few peanuts and marshmallows, unmelted, into mix for a rocky road treat.

To save time, press pretzel mix into a greased 13x9x2-inch baking pan, cool until firm and cut into squares.

POPCORN PARTY MIX

Cyndi's friend Harriet used to bring a large envelope of recipes to share when she visited from Texas. This is a one of those recipes that has been a great hit at sports parties.

6 tablespoons butter
1 tablespoon Worcestershire sauce
1 teaspoon seasoned salt
1/8 teaspoon garlic powder
4 cups or more popped corn, unsalted
1 3-ounce can chow mein noodles
1 1/2 cups wheat cereal squares
1 cup pecan halves
1 teaspoon basil

Preheat oven to 250°. Melt butter. Add Worcestershire sauce, salt and garlic powder; stir until mixed well. In large bowl, gently toss popped corn, chow mein noodles, cereal and pecans together. Drizzle butter mixture over all and toss. Spread onto large baking sheet. Sprinkle with basil. Bake 45 minutes, stirring every 15 minutes. Cool on paper toweling. Serves 8-10.

Per serving: 241 calories; 18.4 fat grams

Instead of using the chow mein noodles, cereal and pecans substitute 1 1/2 cups corn chips, 1 cup stick pretzels and 3 tablespoons diced green chiles. Use the same directions for preparing. Substitute 3/4 cup cheddar cheese for the basil, and bake 15 minutes.

ZESTY SOUTHWESTERN POPCORN

A great treat for popcorn lovers.

20 cups popped popcorn
1/2 cup butter or margarine, melted
4-6 drops hot pepper sauce
1 teaspoon chili powder
1 teaspoon garlic salt
2 tablespoons cilantro, finely chopped
2 tablespoons grated parmesan cheese

Place popcorn in large bowl. Combine remaining ingredients. Drizzle over popcorn and toss until well coated. Serves 20.

Per serving: 98 calories; 7.8 fat grams

CARAMEL CORN

While our children were still in school and we had time to do crafts, we took needlepoint classes from our friend, Gladys. She would serve this wonderful treat when we completed a project.

12 cups popped popcorn
1 cup salted peanuts, almonds or pecans
1 cup brown sugar
1/2 cup butter
1/4 cup light corn syrup
1/2 teaspoon salt
1/2 teaspoon baking soda

Preheat oven to 200°. In large metal or glass pan, combine popcorn and nuts. Set aside. In medium pan, combine sugar, butter, corn syrup and salt. Bring to boil and cook for 5 minutes. Remove from heat and stir in baking soda. Immediately pour over popped corn mixture. Stir gently until most pieces of corn are covered with caramel. Remove to large baking sheet. Bake 45 minutes, stirring every 15 minutes. Serves 12.

Per serving: 256 calories; 16.7 fat grams

1/2 cup popcorn kernels will yield 4 cups of popped popcorn.

PEOPLE CHOW

QUICK to make and always a favorite.

2 cups dry roasted peanuts
1 12-ounce box two-sided wheat/rice cereal
   squares
1/2 cup margarine
1 6-ounce bag semi-sweet chocolate chips
1/2 cup peanut butter
2-3 cups powdered sugar

In large bowl, mix nuts and cereal together. In medium bowl, melt margarine, chocolate chips and peanut butter together in microwave, stirring after each 1 minute until mixture is blended. Pour over cereal mixture and toss until each piece is covered. Add powdered sugar and toss gently until all pieces are covered. Cool and store in airtight container or heavy plastic bags. Serves 12-15.

Per serving: 468 calories; 25.4 fat grams

 Line a coffee can with a plastic bag, fill, tie off and seal can. Keep in your freezer until ready to use.

SUGARED BACON STRIPS

There's nothing nutritious about this appetizer-it is just good.

1 cup brown sugar
1 teaspoon dry mustard, optional
1 pound sliced bacon at room temperature

Preheat oven to 325°. In pie pan, combine brown sugar and mustard. Dip both sides of bacon strips in brown sugar mixture. Place on large baking sheet. Bake 25-30 minutes, turning once, until dark brown. Remove with tongs to paper towel to cool. It will get hard and can be broken into pieces. Serves 8-10.

Per serving: 59 calories; 0.4 fat grams

CHEESE STRAWS

Good as a snack or for dipping.

2 cups cheddar cheese, grated
1/2 cup margarine at room temperature
1 cup flour
1 teaspoon baking powder
1/2 teaspoon salt
1/2 teaspoon cayenne pepper

Preheat oven to 375°. In large mixing bowl, combine all ingredients and blend with pastry blender. Roll into thin logs and cut at intervals to make sticks. Place on sprayed baking sheet. Bake 8-10 minutes or until barely brown. Serves 12.

Per serving: 182 calories; 13.9 fat grams

You can also roll these into small balls, place on baking sheet and flatten with fork to make wafer-type snacks.

Add 1 cup rice cereal to mixture to make a crispier texture. Prepare and bake in same way.

Notes:

Dips and Spreads

ARTICHOKE-BACON DIP

This dip can be served hot or cold.

1 14-ounce can artichoke hearts, drained
   and chopped
4 pieces bacon, fried crisp and crumbled;
   reserve 2 tablespoons for garnish
1 tablespoon onion, finely chopped
1 tablespoon lemon juice
1/2 teaspoon Worcestershire sauce
1/2 cup light mayonnaise
Dash cayenne pepper
Salt and pepper to taste

Preheat oven to 350°. In large bowl, mix all ingredients together. Pour into 8x8-inch baking pan. Bake 10-12 minutes. Serve with cocktail breads or crackers. If not heating, remove to chip and dip dish or bread bowl; surround with crackers or cubed bread. Serves 6-8.

Per serving: 59 calories; 2.4 fat grams

 Lay bacon between paper towels on a paper plate and microwave on high an average of 1 minute per piece to make crispy bacon. Remove with tongs and cool. Cook less if crispy bacon is not preferred.

ASPARAGUS DIP

If there is any of this dip leftover, thin it with milk and serve as a salad dressing.

1 14-ounce can asparagus spears, drained
    and chopped
1/2 cup sour cream
1/4 teaspoon hot pepper sauce
1/2 teaspoon dill weed
1/2 teaspoon beau monde seasoning

In medium bowl, blend all ingredients. Chill. Serve with chips or crackers. Serves 8-10.

Per serving: 36 calories; 3.0 fat grams

Make attractive dip 'dishes' by cutting off the top of green, red or yellow peppers in a fluted design, cleaning out the center and filling with any dip.

BASIC GUACAMOLE

Use this basic recipe to create your own special guacamole.

4 ripe avocados, seeded and peeled
1/4-1/2 cup minced onion
2 tablespoons lemon juice
1/4 cup light mayonnaise or light sour
    cream
1/2 teaspoon garlic salt
Tomatoes

In medium bowl, mash avocados with fork. Add remaining ingredients and mix. If you are not serving immediately, use the mayonnaise to cover the top of the dip. Cover and refrigerate. Then stir it into dip before serving. Garnish with diced tomatoes. Serves 8-10.

Per serving: 103 calories; 9.4 fat grams

 Foot Notes Select firm avocados that feel soft if thumb is lightly pressed into it. Leave in a window sill for one day to soften to right consistency. When ready to use, roll on counter with heel of hand for easier removal from skin. Cut in half, remove seed and scoop out with spoon.

Omit the mayonnaise and/or add any of the following ingredients to our guacamole for your own unique taste: salsa, tomatillos, poblano peppers or green chiles, tomatoes, hot pepper sauce or chili powder.

AVOCADO CRESS DIP

The watercress makes a lighter avocado dip.

2 ripe avocados, softened and peeled
1 cup snipped watercress
2 tablespoons lemon juice
2 tablespoons mayonnaise
1/2 teaspoon salt
1/8 teaspoon ground coriander

In medium bowl, mash avocados. Add remaining ingredients; stir. Garnish with sprig of cilantro. Serve with tortilla chips. Serves 8-10.

Per serving: 76 calories; 7.5 fat grams

We both substitute cumin for the coriander in this recipe.

While refrigerated, place avocado seed in the middle of guacamole to prevent browning. Remove seed to serve.

Coriander has a citrus aroma and taste and is available as seeds or is ground. Cilantro is the fresh leaves of the coriander plant and has a totally different flavor.

AVOCADO CHEESE DIP

The cream cheese makes this a thick and creamy guacamole dip.

2 large avocados, peeled and seeds removed
2 8-ounce packages cream cheese
1 4-ounce can whole green chiles
1 teaspoon garlic salt
2 teaspoons lemon juice

Place all ingredients in blender and mix well. Pour into serving dish. Serve with vegetables, tortilla chips or crackers. Serves 10-12.

Per serving: 191 calories; 18.5 fat grams

 Add hot pepper sauce, chopped jalapeño pepper or cayenne pepper for a spicer taste.

HOT BEAN DIP

The flavor in this recipe is enhanced by the ranch-style beans.

2 jalapeño peppers
1 medium onion
1 clove garlic
1 15-ounce can ranch-style beans, mashed
1/2 cup butter
2 cups sharp cheddar cheese, grated

Chop jalapeño, onion and garlic in food processor. In large microwavable bowl, combine all ingredients. Microwave on high for 1 minute intervals until cheese is melted. Pour into chafing dish. Serve with corn chips, potato chips, bread or crackers. Serves 12-15.

Per serving: 171 calories; 13.3 fat grams

HOT CHEESE AND BROCCOLI DIP

Leftover dip is excellent on baked potatoes or omelets.

4 tablespoons butter or margarine
1 cup onion, chopped
2 garlic cloves, minced
1 cup cubed processed cheese
2 10-ounce packages frozen chopped broccoli, thawed
1 4-ounce can mushroom stems and pieces, drained
1 cup light sour cream
1/4 cup parmesan cheese

In small fry pan, saute onion and garlic in butter. Add cheese and melt, stirring constantly. Add broccoli, mushrooms, sour cream and parmesan cheese. Thin with small amount of milk, if necessary. Serve hot in chafing dish with chips. Serves 30.

Per serving: 48 calories; 3.7 fat grams

 Cyndi substitutes 3 cups chopped fresh broccoli for the frozen broccoli.

CUCUMBER DIP

Enjoy a nice cool, refreshing taste.

1 large unpeeled cucumber, reserving 3
    slices for garnish
1 8-ounce package cream cheese
2 tablespoons lemon juice
2 tablespoons green onions, finely chopped
Salt and pepper

Into a strainer, coarsely grate cucumber, reserving juice. In medium bowl, mix cream cheese and lemon juice. Stir in onions and cucumber. Season to taste with salt and pepper. Thin with reserved cucumber juice, if needed. Spoon into serving dish; garnish with cucumber slices. Chill. Serve with chips and/or fresh vegetables. Serves 10-12.

Per serving: 77 calories; 7.2 fat grams

STROGANOFF DIP WITH MUSHROOMS

1 1/2 pounds fresh mushrooms
1 clove garlic, finely chopped
5 tablespoons butter or margarine
3 tablespoons flour
1 1/4 cups hot water
1 tablespoon beef bouillon (3 cubes)
1/2 teaspoon Worcestershire sauce
1/2 cup sour cream
Parsley

In large skillet, cook mushrooms and garlic in 3 tablespoons butter 5 minutes. Remove mushrooms and set aside. Stir in flour. Add water, bouillon and Worcestershire sauce. Cook until mixture thickens, stirring constantly. Remove from heat and stir in sour cream. Add mushrooms. Serve in warmer or chafing dish. Garnish with parsley. Spear with toothpicks. Serves 6-8.

Per serving: 144 calories; 12.0 fat grams

 Foot Note Freeze and later add leftover dip the next time you make stroganoff.

SUE'S SPINACH DIP

Our friend, Sue, always comes up with great tasting, quick recipes. She serves this wonderful spread at bridge.

1 cup light mayonnaise
1 10-ounce package frozen spinach, thawed
    and drained
2 6-ounce jars marinated artichoke hearts,
    drained and chopped into small and
    medium-sized pieces
1 cup parmesan cheese
1 cup tomatoes, chopped
1/2 cup mozzarella cheese, shredded

Preheat oven to 300°. In large bowl, mix together mayonnaise, spinach, artichoke hearts and parmesan cheese. Pour into 8x8-inch baking dish. Bake 20 minutes. Remove and top with tomatoes and cheese. Serve with crackers or cocktail bread. Serves 8.

Per serving: 131 calories; 6.5 fat grams

IF there is any left over, serve cold as a salad dressing or a sandwich spread.

SPINACH DIP

This all-time favorite disappears quickly.

1 10-ounce package frozen chopped
　　spinach, thawed
1 1/2 cups light sour cream
1 cup light mayonnaise
1 package vegetable soup mix
1 8-ounce can water chestnuts, finely
　　chopped
3 green onions, finely chopped

Squeeze water from spinach. In medium bowl, combine spinach with remaining ingredients. Cover; refrigerate 2 hours. Pour into bread bowl. Also excellent when spread on pumpernickel bread or crackers. Serves 10-12.

Per serving: 78 calories; 2.1 fat grams

 If you should have any left over, mix a small can of tuna into the mixture; it makes a great sandwich filling.

BASIC SPINACH DIP

Can't beat a good basic dip. Georgie always serves this 'holiday staple' in a bread bowl.

1 10-ounce package frozen chopped spinach
1 cup mayonnaise
4 tablespoons instant chopped onion
1 8-ounce can water chestnuts,
    coarsely chopped

Squeeze spinach to remove excess water. In medium bowl, combine other ingredients and chill. Remove to serving dish garnished with curly lettuce; serve with veggies, chips or crackers. Serves 10-12.

Per serving: 167 calories; 16.0 fat grams

 After squeezing juice from spinach, use kitchen shears to QUICKly snip spinach into small pieces. It's much faster than pulling it apart.

DILL WEED DIP

This dip has always been a Duncan favorite served with fresh veggies.

1 cup light sour cream
1 cup light mayonnaise
1/2 tablespoon instant minced onion
2 tablespoons parsley
1 1/2 teaspoons dill weed
1 1/2 teaspoons beau monde
1 1/2 teaspoons Worcestershire sauce
Pinch of salt

Mix all ingredients together and refrigerate until ready to serve. Serves 10-12.

Per serving: 32 calories; 1.6 fat grams

Beau monde is a blend of spices and used as an all-purpose seasoning for cooking or at the table.

Sometimes Cyndi substitutes 1 cup lowfat cottage cheese for half of the sour cream and mayonnaise.

For a QUICKer version, replace sour cream and mayonnaise with prepared ranch dressing.

SALSA

Cyndi makes this in large batches to can or freeze. She makes both chunky and smooth batches.

4 ripe tomatoes (Roma tomatoes make
    thicker salsa; use 6)
1 small onion
3 small green chiles
1/2 clove garlic
1 tablespoon lemon juice
Salt to taste

Put all ingredients in blender and blend to desired consistency. Serves 4.

Per serving: 42 calories; 0.5 fat grams

Use 1 or 2 jalapeño peppers for a spicier salsa.

Make Pico de Gallo by adding 1-2 sprigs of cilantro.

GREEN CHILE CHEESE DIP

3/4 cup light mayonnaise
1/4 cup plain lowfat yogurt
1 cup Monterey Jack cheese, shredded
1 4-ounce can chopped green chiles, drained
1/4 teaspoon red pepper sauce
2 tablespoons green onion, chopped
Salsa

Preheat oven to 350°. In small casserole dish, combine all ingredients. Bake 15 minutes. Garnish with spoonful of salsa. Serve hot with tortilla chips or broken bread. Serves 10-12.

Per serving: 60 calories; 4.0 fat grams

Picante and Pico de Gallo are types of salsa. Commercially, salsa is chunky, picante is smoother and perhaps thicker. Basically, the ingredients are the same and can be thick, thin, smooth or chunky depending on the manufacturer.

CHILI VERDE CON QUESO

This also makes a quick topping for Mexican food or baked potatoes.

1 pound processed cheese
1/4-1/2 cup milk
1 4-ounce can chopped green chiles
1/4 teaspoon salt
1/8 teaspoon garlic powder
1 teaspoon onion powder
2 tablespoons salsa

In medium bowl, combine all ingredients. Microwave on high 2 minutes. Stir and return to microwave for 1 minute intervals until cheese is melted. Serve with tortilla chips or fresh vegetables. Serves 10-12.

Per serving: 164 calories; 13.2 fat grams

Foot Notes

A QUICKer version of this is to melt processed cheese with a 14-ounce can of tomatoes and green chiles. Heat in microwave. If too thin add more cheese; if too thick add a small amount of milk.

Serving in a small slow cooker on low keeps the dip hot and at serving consistency.

TACO PIZZA DIP

3 large avocados, mashed
2 teaspoons lemon juice
1 8-ounce package cream cheese, softened
2 cups light sour cream
1 2-ounce package taco seasoning
1 cup cheddar cheese, shredded
2 medium tomatoes, chopped
1/2 cup black olives, chopped
3 green onions, sliced

Mix avocados and lemon juice; set aside. Beat together cream cheese, sour cream and taco seasoning; set aside. Layer in a large platter or pizza pan: avocado mixture, cream cheese mixture, cheddar cheese, tomatoes, black olives and onions. Serve with plain corn chips. Serves 12.

Per serving: 199 calories; 17.0 fat grams

 For a cold summer 'salad', use leftover taco meat for the first layer and add shredded lettuce before the cheddar cheese. Serve with tortilla chips.

SUPER NACHOS

A great dip served hot or cold. Just omit baking directions.

1 pound lean ground beef
1 package taco seasoning
1 15-ounce can refried beans
1 small onion, chopped
1 pound cheddar cheese, shredded
2 cups light sour cream
1 8-ounce container avocado dip

Preheat oven to 400°. Brown ground beef, drain. Add taco seasoning; mix. In large pizza pan, layer beans, ground beef, onion and cheese. Bake 25 minutes, until heated through and cheese is melted. Layer sour cream and avocado dip over cheese. Serve with corn chips. Serves 12.

Per serving: 402 calories; 31.0 fat grams

Make QUICK nachos with melted cheese spread and salsa to taste. Pour over or dip chips.

TEX-MEX DIP

This layered favorite has been served on many hors d' oeuvre tables.

3 avocados, mashed
1/2 teaspoon salt
1/4 teaspoon pepper
2 teaspoons lemon juice
8 ounces light sour cream
1/2 cup light mayonnaise
1 2-ounce package taco seasoning
19-ounce can jalapeño bean dip
1 cup black olives, chopped
1 cup cheddar cheese, shredded
1 large tomato, chopped

Mix avocados, salt, pepper and lemon juice; set aside. Combine sour cream, mayonnaise and taco seasoning; mix well and set aside. Layer in a large platter or deep pie plate: bean dip, avocado mixture, sour cream mixture, olives, cheddar cheese and tomato. Serve with corn chips. Serves 12.

Per serving: 155 calories; 11.2 fat grams

BLUE CHEESE DIP

Blue cheese is one of Cyndi's favorites. A friend once told her that his grandmother believed that she lived to be 100 years old because she ate a piece of moldy cheese every day. Not really her reason, but . .

2 8-ounce packages cream cheese, cut in
    small pieces
1/2 pound blue cheese, crumbled
1/4 cup drained sweet pickle relish
1 onion, finely chopped
1 tablespoon Worcestershire sauce
1 teaspoon hot pepper sauce
10 dashes cayenne pepper
2 tablespoons light mayonnaise

In large bowl, combine cream cheese and blue cheese. Microwave on high for 1 minute. Continue microwaving and stirring after 30 second intervals until cheese is melted. Add remaining ingredients and beat with mixer until smooth. Chill. If too thick, add small amount of milk. Serve as dip with fresh vegetables. Serves 10-12.

Per serving: 231 calories; 20.5 fat grams

SWISS FONDUE

1 clove garlic, split in half
1 cup dry white wine
1 pound Swiss cheese, grated
1 teaspoon cornstarch
1 teaspoon Worcestershire sauce
1 teaspoon dry mustard

Rub fondue pot with garlic. Discard. Add wine and heat; do not boil. In small bowl, toss cheese with cornstarch and add to wine, half cup at a time. Heat on low until cheese is melted, stirring constantly. Add seasonings. Keep warm on burner. Serve with bread cubes or vegetables. Serves 8-10.

Per serving: 211 calories; 13.9 fat grams

Fondue can be made and served in a slow cooker, keeping warm on low.

BEER-CHEESE FONDUE

2 tablespoons butter or margarine, softened
1/2 small onion, finely chopped
1 tablespoon Worcestershire sauce
1 teaspoon hot pepper sauce
1/4 teaspoon garlic powder
1 1/2 pounds processed American cheese
3/4 cup crumbled blue cheese
1/2 to 1 cup beer
1 unsliced round loaf sourdough, rye
    or egg bread

In medium sauce pan, saute onion in butter 5 minutes. Add Worcestershire sauce, pepper sauce and garlic powder. Reduce heat to medium low and add cheeses, stirring until melted. Add enough beer for desired consistency. Continue to cook, stirring until cheese mixture is entirely melted. Keep warm on fondue stand. Dip bread or vegetables. Serves 15-20.

Per serving: 180 calories; 14.5 fat grams

GOUDA PARTY DIP

A flavorful dip in a unique 'dish'.

1 8-ounce baby Gouda cheese at room
    temperature
1/2 teaspoon prepared mustard
1/2 teaspoon Worcestershire sauce
1/8 teaspoon onion salt
1/8 teaspoon garlic salt

Use scalloped cookie cutter to cut wax from top of
cheese. Carefully remove cheese from shell keeping
shell intact. In mixing bowl, beat cheese until
smooth; add mustard, Worcestershire sauce, onion
salt and garlic salt. Blend well. Refill shell. Serve
with crackers. Serves 6-8.

Per serving: 116 calories; 8.9 fat grams

Another way to serve Gouda cheese
is to slice it in 24 wedges. Spread 12
wedges with favorite spread and top
with remaining twelve wedges.
Secure wedges together with spears
of shrimp, cherry tomato, pickle, or
olive. This is especially good using a
seafood spread.

PEPPERY BEAN DIP

You probably need numb taste buds and good tear ducts to eat this dip.

2 16-ounce cans refried beans
2 cups white cheddar cheese (provolone or
    Monterey jack can be used), shredded
1 cup butter or margarine
4 jalapeño peppers, rinsed, seeded and
    finely chopped
2 tablespoons minced onion
1 clove garlic, finely minced
1 teaspoon jalapeño pepper juice, optional

Combine all ingredients in large double boiler; heat until cheese is melted. Serve hot in a chafing dish with corn chips, tortilla chips or crackers.
Serves 30-40.

Per serving: 101 calories; 7.6 fat grams

For a milder dip, use 2 7-ounce cans green chiles instead of jalapeño peppers.

Use juice from a jar of pickled sliced jalapeños for the jalapeño pepper juice.

MISSISSIPPI CAVIAR

This is a make ahead recipe that can be refrigerated 7-10 days before using.

3 16-ounce cans black-eyed peas, drained
   and rinsed
1 green pepper, diced
1 onion, diced
10 jalapeño peppers, diced
1 3-ounce jar pimiento
1 1/2 teaspoons minced garlic
1 8-ounce bottle herb and spice Italian
   dressing

In large bowl, mix all ingredients together and chill at least overnight. Drain and serve with tortilla chips. Serves 30.

Per serving: 194 calories; 4.3 fat grams

In the south, black eyed peas served on New Years Day bring good luck. They must be the first thing you eat in the new year which is why you often see them served at New Year's Eve parties.

COWBOY CAVIAR

Marilynn, a bridge friend, serves this great dip. It combines interesting, unusual flavors with a colorful presentation.

2 tablespoons red wine vinegar
1 1/2-2 teaspoons hot pepper sauce
1 1/2 teaspoons oil
1 clove garlic, minced
1/8 teaspoon pepper
1 firm, ripe avocado, cubed
1 15-ounce can black-eyed peas
1 15-ounce can corn
2/3 cup thinly sliced onion
1/3-2/3 cup fresh cilantro, chopped
3-4 Roma tomatoes, coarsely chopped
Salt to taste

In large bowl, gently mix all ingredients together. Serve with tortilla chips. Serves 15-18.

Per serving: 129 calories; 2.4 fat grams

 Foot Note To keep from 'crying' when cutting an onion, slice off each end and soak in cold water a short time before chopping or slicing.

HUMMUS

Cyndi's daughters introduced her to hummus while traveling in Australia. They used it on bagels, tortillas, veggie sandwiches and crackers.

1 15-ounce can garbanzo beans, rinsed
    and drained
1 teaspoon sesame seeds
1 clove garlic,
1/4 cup lemon juice
1/2 teaspoon cumin
1/2 teaspoon salt
1/4 teaspoon coarsely ground black pepper
1 teaspoon olive oil
1 tablespoon parsley leaves, chopped
Pinch paprika
1/3 cup water

In food processor, blend all ingredients until smooth. Cover and refrigerate. Serves 8.

Per serving: 109 calories; 4.6 fat grams

 Foot Note Add any combination of the following to vary the recipe: onion, black olives, dried tomatoes, herbs, nuts and/or spinach.

COTTAGE CHEESE DIP

This can also be used as a side dish or a filler for stuffed tomatoes.

1 12-ounce container cottage cheese
2 tablespoons sour cream
1/4 teaspoon onion salt
1/4 teaspoon garlic salt
1/2 teaspoon caraway seed
1/2 teaspoon parsley flakes
1 heaping teaspoon fresh or freeze-dried chives

In large bowl, combine all ingredients. Serve chilled with fresh vegetables. Serves 10-12.

Per serving: 34 calories; 1.2 fat grams

 Foot Note If you prefer, blend the cottage cheese and sour cream together in a food processor or blender.

ORIENTAL DIP

A great starter for a Chinese dinner.

1/3 cup sesame seeds, toasted
1/4 teaspoon ginger
1/4 teaspoon curry powder
2 teaspoons soy sauce
1/2 cup mayonnaise
1 cup sour cream

Toast sesame seeds by placing in a dry frying pan; heat very gently, stirring constantly until golden. Remove from heat; cool. In small bowl, mix remaining ingredients. Stir in sesame seeds. Chill. Serve with sesame wafers. Serves 8-10.

Per serving: 176 calories; 18.1 fat grams

VEGETABLE DIP

Just how quick can a recipe be? Just remember to do this one a day ahead to enhance the flavor. We use this recipe often and serve it in a bread bowl.

1 16-ounce carton sour cream
1 2-ounce package vegetable soup mix

In medium bowl, mix ingredients and chill a day ahead of serving. Serve with bread cubes, potato chips and fresh vegetables. Serves 8-10.

Per serving: 121 calories; 10.8 fat grams

To make a bread bowl, start with small or regular sized sheepherders loaf which is available at most bakeries. Slice off the top half of the loaf. Run knife around edge and lift out the bread. Then you have a 'bowl' in which to serve soup or dips. Cut up the bread and serve on the side. It can be served plain or dipped in butter and toasted in oven or fry pan. For croutons, cut in smaller pieces, dip in favorite butter/herb combination and toast in oven.

CURRIED CHEESE AND BACON DIP

For fewer calories and fat grams substitute plain yogurt cheese for cream cheese.

1 8-ounce package cream cheese at
    room temperature
3/4 cup sour cream
3/4 teaspoon curry powder
3/4 teaspoon garlic powder
1/2 teaspoon chili powder
1/2 teaspoon Worcestershire sauce
5 slices bacon, cooked, drained and
    crumbled
1 tablespoon chopped chives

In small bowl, mix cream cheese, sour cream, curry powder, garlic powder, chili powder and Worcestershire sauce. Stir in bacon and chives, reserving 1 teaspoon bacon and a few chives for garnish. Serve with chips or crackers. Serves 8-10.

Per serving: 151 calories; 14.6 fat grams

Make **Nonfat Yogurt Cheese** by draining yogurt from 24 hours to 4 days before using. Start by lining strainer with 2 layers of cheesecloth, place 1 quart nonfat yogurt into cloth and set in deep pan. Cover strainer and pan with plastic wrap to keep air tight. Periodically drain off whey. Shorter draining produces a moist cheese with more volume. Drain longer for a thicker yogurt cheese with less volume. There are yogurt strainers available through cooking catalogs and gourmet retail outlets. Use in recipes calling for cream cheese.

PEPPERONI DIPPING SAUCE

A taste of your favorite pizzeria.

1 cup pizza sauce
1 clove garlic, minced
1/2 teaspoon Italian seasoning
1/4 cup onion, diced
1/2 cup pepperoni, diced
1/4 cup green pepper, diced

In small saucepan, combine all ingredients. Cook over medium heat until hot. Pour into serving dish. Set in napkin-lined basket filled with warm bread sticks, garlic bread or parmesan crackers. Serves 6-8.

Per serving: 112 calories; 8.7 fat grams

 To make parmesan crackers, lay flour tortillas on large seasoned baking sheet. Spread tortillas with butter; sprinkle with parmesan cheese and parsley. Bake 10 minutes at 350° or until slightly crisp. Cut in wedges.

CHEESY CHILI DIP

Cyndi's brother-in-law sometimes brings this favorite to family events. He spices it up with jalapeños and tomatoes with green chiles.

1 pound processed cheese spread, cubed
1 15-ounce can chili without beans
1 4-ounce can chopped green chilies
1/2 cup onion, finely chopped

Preheat oven to 350°. In large bowl, combine all ingredients. Spoon into medium casserole dish. Bake 20-25 minutes until thoroughly heated. Stir before serving. Serve with toasted bread slices or tortilla chips. Serves 15-20.

Per serving: 53 calories; 3.3 fat grams

 Prepare in the microwave on high 8-10 minutes, stirring every 4 minutes.

DEVILED CHEESE DUNK

A QUICK, zesty ham dip.

1 5-ounce jar pimento cheese spread
1 2 1/4-ounce can deviled ham
1/2 cup light mayonnaise
1/4 cup parsley, chopped
1 tablespoon onion, grated
4 drops hot pepper sauce

In medium bowl, combine ingredients, mixing until smooth. Cover and chill. Serve with potato chips. Serves 6-8.

Per serving: 118 calories; 8.7 fat grams

 Grind leftover beef, turkey, ham or chicken in food processor and substitute for deviled ham. The taste and texture will be much different

ZESTY BEEF DIP

A hearty beef dip with an Italian flavor.

1 pound lean ground beef
1 onion, chopped
1 clove garlic, minced
1 8-ounce can tomato sauce
1/4 cup catsup
1 teaspoon sugar
1/2 teaspoon oregano
1 8-ounce package cream cheese, softened
1/3 cup grated parmesan cheese

In medium fry pan, brown ground beef; drain. Add onion and garlic and cook 5 minutes. Stir in tomato sauce, catsup, sugar and oregano. Cover and simmer gently 10 minutes. Add cream cheese and parmesan cheese, stirring until cream cheese is melted. Serve warm in chafing dish with bread sticks, snack bread and/or crackers. Serves 12.

Per serving: 191 calories; 15.1 fat grams

 Fresh basil is a nice addition to and garnish for this dip.

HOT CRAB DIP

1 10-ounce can cheddar cheese soup
1 8-ounce box processed cheese, cubed
1 4-ounce can chopped ripe olives, drained
1 7-ounce can crab meat, drained and flaked
1 tablespoon lemon juice
1 teaspoon Worcestershire sauce

In medium bowl, microwave soup and cheese on high 2 minutes. Stir. Microwave at 1 minutes intervals until cheese is melted. Add remaining ingredients and mix. Serve warm with toasted bread thins. Serves 12-15.

Per serving: 109 calories; 7.8 fat grams

Foot Note Make your own bread thins by trimming crusts from thin slices of bread. Lightly butter and sprinkle with parmesan cheese and parsley. Cut into fourths. Microwave on high 2 minutes. Microwaving will dry out bread and make it crispier; if you microwave again it will actually toast. Watch carefully so it doesn't burn.

CRAB FONDUE

Georgie's sister-in-law, Cathy, shared this wonderful, creamy crab dip.

1 5-ounce jar processed American cheese
1 8-ounce package cream cheese, cubed
1/4 cup light cream
1 7 1/2-ounce can crabmeat, drained
1/2 teaspoon Worcestershire sauce
1/4 teaspoon garlic salt
1/2 teaspoon cayenne pepper

In fondue pot over low heat, melt cheeses with cream. Add remaining ingredients, stirring constantly. Add more cream if too thick. Serve with bread cubes, vegetables, crackers or tortilla chips. Serves 10-12.

Per serving: 223 calories; 13.4 fat grams

 Foot Notes

Use leftover dip as topping to smother seafood burritos.

This recipe is easily adapted to the slow cooker.

SHRIMP DIP

The seafood sauce adds a colorful presentation and gives this dip a little gusto.

1 3-ounce package cream cheese, at room
    temperature
1/2 cup mayonnaise
1 4-ounce can tiny shrimp, well-drained
1/2 cup celery, finely chopped
1/2 cup green onion, finely chopped
1 1/2 tablespoons lemon juice
1/4 cup seafood sauce

Beat cream cheese and mayonnaise until smooth. Stir in remaining ingredients. Chill. Line serving dish with curly lettuce leaves; spoon seafood sauce on top of lettuce. Pour dip on top and garnish with a few pieces of green onion. Serves 10-12.

Per serving: 119 calories; 10.9 fat grams

 Use any leftover dip in seafood enchiladas. M-m-m, good!

LEMONY FRUIT DIP

This lemon dip makes a refreshing summertime treat.

1 8-ounce package reduced fat cream
    cheese at room temperature
1/2 cup light sour cream
1/4 cup frozen lemonade concentrate,
    thawed
2 tablespoons sugar
2 teaspoons grated lemon rind
Cut-up fresh fruit

In medium bowl, combine all ingredients except fruit; blend well. Cover and refrigerate at least 30 minutes while preparing fruit. Use wooden picks to spear fruit to dip. Serves 8-10.

Per serving: 88 calories; 4.7 fat grams

 Make fruit kabobs on a long wooden pick and spoon dip over them. Making the kabobs will take more time, but what a nice presentation they make on a cheese platter.

ORANGE DIP FOR FRESH FRUIT

Serve this elegant dip with any meal, winter or summer.

4 eggs
1/3 cup butter or margarine, at room
    temperature
1/4 cup sugar
4 teaspoons grated fresh orange rind
1/8 teaspoon salt
1/2 cup orange juice
1 teaspoon lemon juice
1 small pineapple
2 medium apples
2 oranges or 1 grapefruit or a combination
    of both
2 bananas

In blender, combine eggs, butter, sugar, orange rind and salt. Blend 1 minute. Gradually add orange and lemon juices while running on low. Pour mixture into medium saucepan. Using very low heat, cook until thickened, stirring constantly to prevent lumps from forming. Remove and cool. Chill while preparing fruit. Serves 8-10.

Per serving: 202 calories; 9.3 fat grams

Dip bananas and apples in lemon juice before arranging on fruit platter. Georgie adds a bit of sugar to lemon juice before dipping fruit.

When in season, red and green grapes or strawberries are a colorful addition to a fruit platter. For frosted grapes, dip in lemon juice and roll in sugar.

MARSHMALLOW FRUIT DIP

Strawberries, sliced bananas and pineapple chunks are especially good with this dip.

2 cups marshmallow creme
1/2 cup mayonnaise
2 teaspoons grated orange peel
4 teaspoons orange juice
2 1/2 teaspoons lemon juice

In blender, combine all ingredients. Blend until smooth. Pour into serving dish. Set in the middle of a platter with an assortment of cut-up fruit pierced with toothpick for easy dipping. Serves 8-10.

Per serving: 169 calories; 9.8 fat grams

 Substitute 2-3 cups of low fat yogurt for marshmallow creme and mayonnaise for a lower calorie/fat gram count.

CHEESECAKE DIP

A great double dip for strawberry cheesecake lovers.

1 8-ounce package light cream cheese at
    room temperature
2/3 cup light sour cream
6 tablespoons powdered sugar
2 tablespoons milk
1/3 teaspoon almond extract
1 quart fresh strawberries
1/2 cup graham cracker crumbs

In mixing bowl, beat cream cheese until smooth. Add sour cream, sugar, milk and extract; mix until smooth. Transfer to serving bowl. Place both cheesecake dip and bowl of graham cracker crumbs in center of large serving platter. Arrange strawberries around the bowl. Dip strawberries into cheesecake mixture, then into crumbs. Serves 8.

Per serving: 118 calories; 6.0 fat grams

For a really QUICK fruit dip, beat 1 3 1/2-ounce package instant vanilla pudding and 1 1/2 cups milk until well blended. Fold in 1 cup sour cream, 1/4 cup orange juice and 1 teaspoon grated orange peel. Chill.

CHOCOLATE FONDUE

Chocolate lovers heaven!

6 1-ounce squares unsweetened chocolate
1 1/2 cups sugar
1 cup light cream
1/2 cup butter or margarine
1/2 teaspoon salt
3 tablespoons creme de cacao or
   orange-flavored liqueur

In medium saucepan, melt chocolate over low heat. Add sugar, cream, butter and salt. Cook, stirring constantly, about 5 minutes or until thickened. Stir in liqueur. Pour into fondue pot. Keep warm over burner. Spear fruit and dip. Serves 12-14.

Per serving: 267 calories; 17.8 fat grams

 In addition to fruit, try dipping angel food or pound cake, marsh-mallows, maraschino cherries, and frozen bananas.

PEANUT BUTTER LOG

This is a good, healthy snack for a brunch and for children.

1/2 cup peanut butter
2 tablespoons honey
3 1/2 tablespoons instant milk
1/2 cup coconut
2-3 apples, sliced

In medium bowl, mix peanut butter, honey and milk together. Place coconut on waxed paper. Spoon peanut mixture on top of coconut and shape into ball. Refrigerate. Spread on apple slices. Serves 8-10.

Per serving: 143 calories; 8.9 fat grams

 Add other nutritional items like raisins, wheat germ or chocolate chips. Roll in peanuts or sunflower seeds.

CHEESE LOG

Turn a commercial cheese spread into a tasty, attractive cheese log.

1 8-ounce package cream cheese
1 6-ounce container cold pack sharp
    cheddar cheese spread
Garlic salt to taste
1 tablespoon pimiento
1/2 cup walnuts, finely chopped

Mix all ingredients; chill. Shape into log; roll in walnuts. Serves 6-8.

Per serving: 229 calories; 21.3 fat grams

 Substitute other cold pack cheese spreads. We find the wine cheese spread particularly flavorful.

BAKED BRIE

The garlic and butter in this recipe make it very rich and decadent.

1/2 cup butter
2 cloves garlic, chopped
1 round of Brie
1 prepared pie crust

Preheat oven to 350°. In glass pie plate, melt butter in microwave. Sprinkle garlic on Brie and wrap with pie crust. Place in pan with butter. Spoon butter over crust. Bake 15-20 minutes until crust is browned. Serve with crackers or cocktail bread. Serves 12-15.

Per serving: 153 calories; 13.1 fat grams

Brie is good served cold without any seasonings.

For QUICK Brie, omit the pie crust and bake 5-10 minutes.

GEORGIE'S ABSOLUTE FAVORITE CHEESE BALL

Georgie was given this recipe by Mary many years ago when they were teaching in Fort Collins, and it has become a much requested family favorite and gift item.

2 8-ounce packages cream cheese, softened
8 ounces sharp cheddar cheese, shredded
1 tablespoon pimento, chopped
1 tablespoon green pepper, chopped
1 tablespoon onion flakes
2 teaspoons Worcestershire sauce
1 teaspoon lemon juice
1 dash cayenne
1 dash salt
1/2 cup pecans, finely chopped

Combine all ingredients except pecans. Mix until well blended. Divide into two parts; shape into balls or logs and roll in pecans. Chill. Serve with wheat crackers. Serves 10-12.

Per serving: 226 calories; 21.1 fat grams

Foot Notes

Cheese balls can be frozen, but they will be crumbly.

Unless the recipe states differently, use sharp cheddar cheese for cheese balls. Avoid using longhorn cheddar which does not blend well

SMOKEY CHEESE BALL

1 8-ounce package cream cheese, softened
1 1/2 cups mild cheddar cheese, grated
1 5-ounce jar smoke flavored processed
    cheese spread
1 teaspoon Worcestershire sauce
1/2 teaspoon dry mustard
1/2 teaspoon salt
3/4 cup black olives, chopped
1/4 cup parsley, chopped

Blend cheeses, Worcestershire sauce, mustard and salt until smooth. Fold in olives; shape into ball. Roll in parsley. Chill. Serves 10-12.

Per serving: 181 calories; 15.9 fat grams

 For a change of taste, use a different flavor processed cheese spread.

BLUE CHEESE BALL

1 8-ounce package cream cheese
4 ounces blue cheese, crumbled
1/4 cup margarine
2/3 cup black olives, chopped
1 tablespoon chives, chopped
1/2 cup walnuts, chopped

Combine all ingredients; mix well. Shape into ball and roll in walnuts. Serve with an assortment of crackers. Serves 8-10.

Per serving: 208 calories; 20.4 fat grams

Cyndi adjusts this recipe by adding 1 cup cheddar cheese, 1 teaspoon Worcestershire sauce, 1/4 teaspoon cayenne pepper and omitting the olives.

PINEAPPLE CHEESE BALL

We cut out recipes; we collect recipes from our friends; we make up recipes and write them down; then they get lost somehow. Well, Georgie has searched for this recipe, found it and, boy, are we lucky.

2 8-ounce packages cream cheese, softened
1 8 1/2 ounce can crushed pineapple,
    drained
2 cups pecans, chopped
1/4 cup green pepper, finely chopped
2 tablespoons onion flakes
1 teaspoon salt

Set aside 1 cup pecans. Combine remaining ingredients; mix well. Shape into ball and roll in reserved pecans. Garnish with pineapple slices and maraschino cherries. Serve with assorted crackers. Serves 16-20.

Per serving: 140 calories; 13.1 fat grams

 This cheese ball is delicious served with fruit, nut or rye bread. Try different fruits, like apples, apricots or peaches, in it.

PICKLE CHEESE BALL

This cheese ball can be made up to a week ahead of serving; aging improves the flavor.

1/2 cup prepared cheese spread
1 cup English sharp cheese spread
3 8-ounce packages cream cheese
1/4 cup sweet pickle relish
1/2 cup walnuts or parsley

Combine all ingredients; mix well. Shape into ball and roll in chopped nuts or parsley. Serve with crackers. Serves 18-20.

Per serving: 163 calories; 15.3 fat grams

 Make individual cheese balls by rolling cheese mixture into small balls and rolling in nuts or parsley. Spear with wooden pick. Stick into whole apples or pears and set on serving tray with fruit and cracker arrangement.

BUSY COOK'S CHEESE BALL

This cheese mixture is divided into three balls and rolled in favorite combinations. They make a great gift basket filled with packages of crackers. Prepare ahead to take to special gatherings.

1 8-ounce package cream cheese, softened
4 cups cheddar cheese, shredded
2 tablespoons milk
2 tablespoons onion, finely chopped
2 tablespoons Worcestershire sauce
3-4 tablespoons coarse ground black pepper, or multi-colored ground pepper
1/2 cup blue cheese, crumbled
3-4 tablespoons parsley
1/4 teaspoon garlic powder
1/3 cup pecans, chopped

In large mixer bowl, beat cream cheese, cheddar cheese, milk, onion and Worcestershire sauce until fluffy. Divide into three portions and place each on a piece of plastic wrap or waxed paper. Shape one cheese ball and roll in ground pepper. Mix the second cheese portion with blue cheese, shape and roll in parsley. Mix the garlic powder into the third cheese portion and roll in pecans. Wrap each cheese ball tightly with plastic wrap, place in plastic bag and store in refrigerator until ready to use. Each cheese ball serves 6-8.

Per serving:
Ground pepper: 130 calories; 10.9 fat grams
Blue cheese: 161 calories; 13.3 fat grams
Pecans: 146 calories;12.7 fat grams

Foot Note Use an extra inexpensive coffee grinder, to get a quantity of fresh-ground pepper QUICKly, The coffee grinder is also handy to grind other spices.

CRAB-CHEESE BALL

6-ounces snow crab meat
1 8-ounce package cream cheese
2 teaspoons chopped chives
1/4 teaspoon garlic powder
1/4 teaspoon salt
1/2 cup pecans, chopped

Mix all ingredients together. Shape into log or ball and roll in pecans. Serve with crackers and/or vegetables. Serves 8-10

Per serving: 128 calories; 11.2 fat grams

Add 1/4 cup finely chopped celery or 1/4 cup finely chopped green pepper for extra crunch.

For a really QUICK seafood spread, place an 8-ounce brick of cream cheese in center of small serving plate, pour a small jar of cocktail sauce over and around the brick, crumble crab or shrimp over the top. Serve with crackers.

SMOKED SALMON BALL

Georgie reminds us to keep a can of salmon in our pantries or a small package of smoked salmon in the freezer for a QUICK appetizer.

1 14-ounce can salmon, drained
1 8-ounce package cream cheese
1/4 teaspoon liquid smoke
2 teaspoons horseradish
2 teaspoons lemon juice
2 teaspoons onion juice
1/2 teaspoon salt
1/2 cup pecans, finely chopped

In medium bowl, mix all ingredients, except pecans together. Refrigerate 20 minutes before forming into ball. Form a ball and roll in nuts. Refrigerate. Serve with crackers. Serves 8-10.

Per serving: 171 calories; 13.6 fat grams

 Foot Notes If you don't have onion juice on hand, use grated onion.

Set out smoked salmon and crackers for an extra QUICK hors d'oeuvre.

DRIED BEEF CHEESE BALL

Dried beef is a versatile addition to cheese dips, salads, sandwiches and sauces.

3 8-ounce packages cream cheese
2 5-ounce jars dried beef, finely chopped
1 bunch green onions, tops included,
    chopped
2 tablespoons Worcestershire sauce

Combine all ingredients except 1/4 dried beef. Shape into ball; roll in reserved dried beef and refrigerate at least 4 hours to enhance flavor. Serves 15.

Per serving: 194 calories; 16.6 fat grams

For a very fine texture, use your food processor to chop dried beef. Kitchen shears work great to snip beef if you prefer it coarser.

CHICKEN-CHEESE LOG

The steak sauce and curry give this cheese ball its zip. The almonds add crunch and compliment the chicken.

2 8-ounce packages cream cheese, softened
1 tablespoon steak sauce
1/2 teaspoon curry
1 1/2 cups chicken, finely chopped
1/2 cup celery, minced
1/4 cup parsley, chopped
1/4 cup toasted almonds, chopped

Combine all ingredients except 1/2 parsley and almonds; mix well. Shape into log. Combine reserved parsley and almonds. Roll log in mixture. Serve with crackers. Serves 14-16.

Per serving: 149 calories; 13.1 fat grams

For ease in forming log or ball, wrap in plastic wrap and refrigerate mixture 4 hours before shaping and rolling to coat.

HAM AND CHEESE BALL

This delightfully tasty spread is best when served on thin wheat crackers.

1 8-ounce package cream cheese
1/4 cup mayonnaise
2 cups cooked ham, finely ground
2 tablespoons parsley, chopped
1 teaspoon minced onion
1/4 teaspoon dry mustard
1/4 teaspoon hot pepper sauce
1/2 cup pecans, chopped

Combine all ingredients, except pecans. Mix well. Shape into ball; roll in pecans. Serve with thin wheat crackers. Serves 12-15.

Per serving: 185 calories; 16.9 fat grams

 If serving a large crowd, divide cheese mixture into two or three portions, roll in balls or logs, place on smaller platters and surround with crackers. Set around a room so all guests have a chance to sample.

ZESTY ARTICHOKE SPREAD

This has always been one of our favorites.

2 14-ounce cans artichoke hearts, drained
    and chopped
1 cup parmesan cheese
1 cup mayonnaise
Dash garlic salt
Dash Worcestershire sauce
Dash hot pepper sauce

Preheat oven to 350°. In large bowl, combine all ingredients. Spoon into lightly greased baking dish. Bake 20 minutes. Serve with crackers. Serves 10-12.

Per serving: 213 calories; 18.2 fat grams

 Grate bricks of fresh parmesan cheese on top of dips or salads. The firm cheese adds a pleasant texture and flavor to food.

ARTICHOKE SURPRISE

Another great recipe that moved to Greeley with Georgie. There are many variations and all winners.

1 14-ounce can artichoke hearts in water,
   drained
1 8-ounce jar marinated artichokes, drained
1 4-ounce can chopped green chiles
6 tablespoons salad dressing or mayonnaise
1 1/2 cups colby cheese, shredded

Chop artichokes and place in bottom of baking dish. Spread chiles on top. Cover with mayonnaise and top with cheese. Bake 20 minutes. Serve with tortilla chips. Serves 8-12.

Per serving: 128 calories; 7.9 fat grams

Foot Note

Leftover Artichoke Surprise makes a delicious sauce for pasta. Add spinach, sautéed onions and red or yellow peppers, if desired. Mix it with eggs to make an omelet or with hash browned potatoes to make a wonderful side dish.

SAUERKRAUT SPREAD

Prepare this spread at least 2 days before serving time. The taste is so subtle that you will not even know that there is sauerkraut in it.

2 1/2 cups sauerkraut, drained well and
    finely chopped
2 cups sharp cheddar cheese, grated
2 or 3 green onions, finely chopped
3 tablespoons green pepper, finely chopped
1 hard boiled egg, finely chopped
1 cup fine dry bread crumbs
1/4 cup light mayonnaise
1 tablespoon sugar
Pinch salt

In large bowl, mix all ingredients together. Pour into molded pan. Refrigerate 2 days before planning to serve. Unmold on lettuce lined serving tray and surround with crackers. Serves 15-20.

Per Serving: 99 calories; 5.1 fat grams

Foot Note Small shaped pottery dishes, bundt pan or large shaped bowl can be used. Prepare with cooking spray.

VEGETABLE TORTE

Make this attractive spread the day before a scheduled shindig.

1 1-ounce packet ranch dressing mix
2 8-ounce packages cream cheese, softened
1 6-ounce jar marinated artichoke hearts,
　　drained and chopped
1/3 cup cup roasted red peppers, drained
　　and chopped
3 tablespoons parsley

In large bowl, combine ranch dressing and cream cheese. In small bowl, combine artichoke hearts, red pepper and parsley. Line a 3-cup bowl with plastic wrap. Layer cheese and vegetable mixtures, beginning and ending with a cheese layer. Chill at least 4 hours. To serve, invert on plate lined with a leafy lettuce leaf. Remove plastic wrap. Garnish with pimiento and parsley. Serve with crackers. Serves 10-12.

Per serving: 161 calories; 14.6 fat grams

In place of the artichokes, use broccoli, onions, carrots and celery chopped finely in the food processor.

SEAFOOD SPREAD

Serve this hot or cold.

1 8-ounce package cream cheese at room
    temperature
1/2 cup mayonnaise
1 8-ounce package crabmeat or 1 7-ounce
    can crabmeat
2 green onions, chopped
1-2 drops hot pepper sauce
1/2 teaspoon Worcestershire sauce
1/2 cup sliced almonds

Preheat oven to 350°. In medium bowl, mix cream cheese and mayonnaise. Add remaining ingredients, except almonds. Pour into baking dish and top with almonds. Bake 25 minutes. Serve with crackers or cocktail bread. Serves 8-10.

Per serving: 230 calories; 20.5 fat grams

Variations:
Use shrimp in place of crab, add 1 tablespoon horseradish and top with walnuts.

Use smoked salmon in place of crab and 1 tablespoon lemon juice in place of Worcestershire sauce.

CRAB SPREAD

This is a perfect QUICK hors d'oeuvre from the kitchen of our friend, Marty.

1 8-ounce package cream cheese, softened
1/2 teaspoon salt
1/4 teaspoon garlic powder
1 tablespoon lemon juice
1 7 1/2-ounce can flaked crab
1/2 cup seafood cocktail sauce

In medium bowl, mix cream cheese, salt, garlic powder and lemon juice together. Fold in crab. Shape in mound on top of lettuce leaf. Pour cocktail sauce over it. Serve with rye crackers. Serves 8-10.

Per serving: 124 calories; 9.1 fat grams

Substitute tuna and 1/4 cup ranch dressing or chicken and 1/2 cup picante sauce for crab and cocktail sauce.

CRAB ROYALE

Horseradish in this recipe adds a nice tangy flavor.

1 cup half and half cream
2 3-ounce packages cream cheese at room
    temperature
1 small onion, chopped
1 tablespoon light mayonnaise
2 teaspoons horseradish
1/2 teaspoon lemon juice
1/2 teaspoon Worcestershire sauce
1/2 teaspoon parsley
1/2 teaspoon garlic salt
1/2 teaspoon onion salt
1/4 teaspoon pepper
1/2 teaspoon hot pepper sauce
2 6-ounce cans crab meat, drained

In large bowl, mix cream and cream cheese together. Add remaining ingredients and mix. Microwave 1 minute; stir. Continue microwaving at 1 minute intervals until warmed through. Serve warm with crackers. Serves 12.

Per serving: 111 calories; 7.7 fat grams

Foot Note
The only fat you get from crab is what you add to it. It has very few calories.

EASY, EASY TINY SHRIMP SPREAD

Guaranteed not to take longer than 5 minutes from start to finish. The hardest task is opening the cream cheese package.

1 4-ounce can tiny shrimp, drained
1 tablespoon lemon juice
1 cup bottled seafood cocktail sauce
1 8-ounce package cream cheese

In small bowl, mix shrimp, lemon juice and seafood sauce together. Place cream cheese block on serving plate. Pour shrimp mixture on top. Surround with crackers. Serves 8-10.

Per serving: 127 calories; 9.1 fat grams

 Prepare this for a 4th of July theme party and serve with blue corn chips. Voilá! It's red, white and blue.

TUNA MELT

Tuna and dill compliment each other in this layered spread.

2 6-ounce cans chunk white tuna in water, drained
4 cups fresh spinach, finely chopped
1 cup celery, finely chopped
6 green onions, finely chopped
1 1/2 teaspoons dill
2 teaspoons lemon juice
1/2 cup light mayonnaise
1 1/2 cups mozzarella cheese

Preheat oven to 350°. In large bowl, separate tuna. Add remaining ingredients, except 1/2 cup cheese. Pour into baking dish and top with remaining 1/2 cup cheese. Bake 15-20 minutes, until bubbly. Serve with whole wheat party bread thins or crackers. Serves 12.

Per serving: 106 calories; 4.8 fat grams

DRIED BEEF SPREAD

Georgie brought this recipe with her when she moved to Greeley. It was another winner from the kitchen of her friend, Sally.

1 8-ounce package cream cheese
1/2 cup sour cream
1/4 cup green pepper, chopped
2 tablespoons onion flakes
2 tablespoons milk
1 3-ounce package dried beef, cut into
    small pieces
1/2 teaspoon pepper
1/2 cup pecans, chopped
Garlic salt to taste, optional

Preheat oven to 350°. In medium bowl, combine all ingredients except pecans. Pour into casserole dish. Sprinkle pecans on top of cheese mixture. Bake 15-20 minutes. Serve with tortilla chips. Serves 8-10.

Per serving: 158 calories; 14.1 fat grams

 Foot Note Instead of using chopped pecans, brown 1/2 cup pecan halves in 2 teaspoons butter and a pinch of salt. Spread on top of dip and bake.

TURKEY SPREAD WITH CURRY

Bake this in a zucchini boat as an entree.

1 1/2 cups cooked turkey, finely chopped
1 hard-cooked egg, chopped
1 cup light mayonnaise
1 clove garlic minced
1/2 cup celery, finely chopped
1 tablespoon minced onion,
3/4 teaspoon curry powder
1/3 teaspoon salt
1/3 teaspoon lemon juice
1 2-ounce jar sliced pimientos, drained and
    chopped

In large bowl, combine all ingredients. Blend well. Cover and chill. Serve with crackers and a mound of red and green grapes. Serves 12.

Per serving: 61 calories; 2.7 fat grams

 Use this as a filler for celery or on a bed of lettuce as a luncheon salad.

Spreads
Page 103

Notes:

Cold Hors d'oeuvres

COOL GARDEN PIZZA

Fresh vegetables put this pizza at the top of any gardener's list of easy-to prepare snacks. Don't let the number of ingredients scare you. This is still a quick and easy recipe and serves a crowd.

2 8-ounce cans refrigerated crescent rolls
1 8-ounce carton light sour cream
1-2 tablespoons horseradish
1/4 teaspoon salt
Dash pepper
2 cups fresh mushrooms, stemmed and sliced
1 cup Roma tomatoes, chopped
1 cup broccoli, broken into small florets
1/2 cup green pepper, chopped
1/2 cup cucumber, seeded and chopped
1/2 cup green onions, chopped
1/2 cup black olives, sliced

Preheat oven to 350°. Separate crescent roll dough into four long rectangles and spread onto 15x10x1-inch baking pan or large baking stone. Pinch seams together. Bake 10-12 minutes until lightly brown. Remove and cool completely. Blend sour cream, horseradish, salt and pepper together. Spread mixture over cooled crust. Top with vegetables in order listed. Cut into 50-60 small squares. Refrigerate. Serves 28.

Per serving: 63 calories; 2.7 fat grams

For a different taste, combine 2 8-ounce packages of cream cheese, 1 1/2 tablespoons light mayonnaise, 1 tablespoon dill weed, and salt and pepper to taste. Substitute for sour cream mixture.

Use food processor to speed up vegetable preparation.

FRUIT PIZZA

This is an attractive and refreshing addition to a party table. This may take a little longer to put together, but it is well worth the effort.

1 12-ounce package sugar cookie dough
3/4 cup water
1/2 cup orange juice
1/2 cup pineapple juice, drained from fruit
3 tablespoons lemon juice
3 tablespoons cornstarch
1/4 cup sugar
1 8-ounce package light cream cheese
1 teaspoon vanilla
1/2 cup powdered sugar
2 tablespoons pineapple juice, drained
    from fruit
1 8-ounce can crushed pineapple, drained,
    juice reserved
2 bananas, sliced
1 8-ounce package strawberries, sliced
1 cup red or green grapes or
    combination, sliced
3-4 kiwi fruit, peeled and sliced
1 12-ounce can mandarin oranges, drained

Preheat oven to 400°. Spray large round pizza pan. Spread cookie dough evenly into pan. Bake 8-10 minutes until slightly browned; remove and cool. In medium sauce pan combine water, orange juice, 1/2 cup pineapple juice, lemon juice, cornstarch and sugar. Heat until thickened. Set aside to cool. In medium bowl, combine cream cheese, vanilla, powdered sugar and 2 tablespoons pineapple juice. Spread onto cooled crust. Spread pineapple over cream cheese. Arrange remaining fruit in design or in layers on top of pineapple. Pour cooled sauce over top of fruit, spreading with back of spoon to seal edges. Refrigerate. Cut into 20-25 small slices. Serves 12.

Per serving: 305 calories; 12.7 fat grams

 Foot Note If a less sweet crust is desired, line pan with pie crust and press chopped walnuts or pecans into it. Follow the above directions eliminating the sugar cookie dough.

SPICE MIX DIP FOR BREAD

Throughout Cyndi's Australian travels, this was a popular starter to meals. This is her favorite combination of herbs and spices.

1 tablespoon sliced almonds
1/4 cup sesame seeds
4 teaspoons oregano
1/2 teaspoon seasoning salt
3/4 teaspoon curry powder
1/2 teaspoon cumin
1/4 teaspoon fresh ground black pepper
Dash cayenne

In food processor, chop almonds until finely ground. In small fry pan, toast all ingredients 1-3 minutes until spices are fragrant and turn golden brown, stirring constantly. To serve, add olive oil or serve olive oil on the side with crusty bread. Serves 6-8.

Per Serving: 44 calories; 3.8 fat grams

Crusty breads such as Foccacia, French, Italian or baguettes are best with this dip.

STUFFED CELERY

Many varieties of fillings make stuffed celery an easy to serve hors d'oeuvre.

Shrimp-Pineapple Filling
    1 4-ounce can shrimp, drained and
        chopped
    1/3 cup light mayonnaise
    1/4 cup crushed pineapple, drained
    1 tablespoon chopped walnuts
    1 tablespoon minced parsley
    1 1/2 teaspoons lemon juice
    1 1/2 teaspoons onion, finely chopped
    1/4 teaspoon salt
    Dash hot pepper sauce

Almond-Cream Cheese Filling
    1 3-ounce package cream cheese at
        room temperature
    1/4 cup toasted almonds, finely
        chopped
    1 tablespoon chili sauce
    1/2 teaspoon curry powder
    Dash salt

Easy, Easy Filling
    2 4-ounce jars pimiento cheese spread

In medium bowl, combine all ingredients for selected filling; stuff celery stalks and cut into 2-3 inch pieces. Serves 8-10.

Per serving:
Shrimp-Pineapple: 30 calories; 0.8 fat grams
Almond-Cream Cheese: 57 calories; 5.3 fat grams
Easy, Easy: 95 calories; 7.9 fat grams

All of our cheese balls and cold spreads make great celery stuffers.

Wrap celery in foil and store in refrigerator. It will stay crispy and last longer.

Cold Hors d'oeuvres

OPEN-FACE CUCUMBER SQUARES

Our friend Ann serves these simply delicious tidbits at bridge gatherings.

2 8-ounce cartons cream cheese
4 teaspoons ranch salad dressing mix
24 slices cocktail-size pumpernickel
    rye bread
4-5 medium cucumbers, peeled if desired,
    thinly sliced
Dill weed

In small bowl, combine cream cheese and salad dressing mix. Spread on one side of each slice of bread. Top with cucumber slice and sprinkle with dill weed (a small sprig of fresh dill can be substituted). Serves 12.

Per serving: 189 calories; 13.9 fat grams

MARINATED MUSHROOMS

An easy-to-prepare ahead recipe. Don't let the number of ingredients scare you off.

1 1/2 pounds fresh small whole mushrooms
1 cup olive oil
1 stalk celery with leaves, chopped
1 clove garlic, peeled
2 tablespoons lemon juice
1 tablespoon white vinegar
8 peppercorns
3/4 teaspoon oregano
1/4 teaspoon salt
1/2 teaspoon rosemary
1/2 teaspoon thyme
1/2 teaspoon sage
1/2 bay leaf
1/4 teaspoon celery seed

In large saucepan, combine all ingredients and bring to boil. Simmer 5 minutes, stirring occasionally. Pour into glass bowl; cover, refrigerate and marinate several hours or overnight. To serve, drain and place in serving bowl. Spear with wooden picks. Serves 8-10.

Per Serving: 157 calories; 14.1 fat grams

Foot Notes

A QUICKer version: Pour 1 16-ounce bottle Italian dressing with lots of spices over 1 15-ounce can drained black olives, 1 8-ounce carton fresh mushrooms, and 1 15-ounce can artichoke hearts.

Use marinade from either version to marinate steaks or chicken. Discard after marinating meat. Grill vegetables in wire basket if desired.

CHEESE STUFFED MUSHROOMS

1 pound medium fresh mushrooms
2 cups water
1 tablespoon lemon juice
1 8-ounce package cream cheese
1/2 cup walnuts, finely chopped
1 teaspoon Worcestershire sauce
1/2 teaspoon curry powder
Fresh parsley sprigs
Paprika

In large saucepan, bring water and lemon juice to boil. Add whole mushrooms. Simmer 2 minutes, drain and cool. Remove stems from mushrooms, chop finely and reserve 1/2 cup for filling. In small bowl blend cream cheese with walnuts, Worcestershire sauce and curry powder. Stir in mushroom stems. Place sprig of parsley in each mushroom cavity and fill with cheese mixture. Sprinkle with paprika. Chill 2-3 hours before serving. Serves 10-12.

Per Serving: 92 calories; 8.2 fat grams

 For hot mushrooms, reserve the parsley sprig as a garnish after baking. Bake 10 minutes at 400°.

DEVILED EGGS

An all-time favorite with a variety of creative fillings which can be piped from a decorator bag into the cavity to make them look fancier.

12 hard-boiled eggs, cut in half lengthwise
4-5 tablespoons light mayonnaise (Georgie
    uses salad dressing)
3/4 teaspoon salt
1/2 teaspoon pepper
1/2 teaspoon sugar
1 1/2 tablespoons vinegar (Georgie uses
    sweet pickle relish)
1 1/2 tablespoons mustard

In small bowl, place egg yolks. Save egg whites. Mash yolks with mayonnaise until smooth. Add remaining ingredients. Refill egg whites. Garnish with paprika, olives, pimiento, or dill weed. Serves 8-12.

Per Serving: 89 calories; 5.9 fat grams

 Foot Notes Try any of these additions to deviled eggs: celery, green pepper, ham pieces, bacon, crab, chicken, avocado, chile peppers and/or lemon juice.

To make these little 'devils' act like 'angels' and stay put on the platter, cut off a thin slice on the bottom of each deviled egg.

SHRIMP STUFFED EGGS

8 hard-boiled eggs, cut in half lengthwise
2 tablespoons mayonnaise
1 cup cooked shrimp, chopped
2 tablespoons celery, minced
2 tablespoons onion, minced
2 tablespoons sweet pickle relish

In small bowl, place egg yolks. Save egg whites on plate. Mash yolks with mayonnaise until smooth. Add remaining ingredients. Refill egg whites. Garnish with paprika, olives, pimiento, or dill weed. Serves 8-12.

Per serving: 92 calories; 6.1 fat grams

 To keep egg shells from cracking while boiling, add a pinch of salt to the water before bringing to a boil.

TACO CHICKEN WRAPS

Wraps are popular as starters with salsa or as luncheon 'sandwiches'.

1 red pepper, cut in 1/4-inch strips
1 yellow onion, cut in 1/4-inch strips
1 2-ounce package taco seasoning
2 tablespoons vegetable oil
1 15-ounce can black beans
1 14-ounce can tomatoes with green chiles,
    undrained
4 chicken breasts, cooked and diced
1 1/2 cups cooked rice
1 1/2 cups Monterey Jack cheese, grated
6 10-inch flour tortillas

In skillet, saute pepper and onion with taco seasoning in oil 5 minutes. Add beans, tomatoes, chicken and rice. Heat through until liquid is evaporated. Assemble by dividing mixture among tortillas and topping with cheese. Roll up each tortilla tightly and secure with toothpick. Wrap each in plastic wrap. Chill. When ready to serve, remove plastic wrap and cut each into 3-4 pieces. Place on serving tray around a dish of salsa. Serves 10-12.

Per serving: 323 calories; 10.1fat grams

Foot Notes Chilling makes slicing the wraps easier. To chill QUICKly, place in freezer for a short time.

Refried, white or red beans can be substituted for black beans.

TORTILLA ROLL-UPS

There are so many fillings for tortilla roll-ups. This one is mild but tangy.

1 8-ounce package cream cheese at room
    temperature
10 sun-dried tomato halves, packed in herb-
    seasoned olive oil, drained and chopped
1 5-ounce container spreadable cheese with
    pepper (can be flavored cream cheese
    or cold pack cheese)
1/3 cup packed fresh basil leaves, chopped
4 large flour tortillas

In medium bowl, mix all ingredients except tortillas until blended. Spread evenly on tortillas. Roll each tortilla tightly, jelly-roll fashion. Wrap each roll in plastic wrap and refrigerate at least 4 hours. To serve, unwrap, trim ends and cut into 1/2-inch slices. Serves 20-24.

Per serving: 186 calories; 13.3 fat grams

 Try tortillas with a seafood filling, green chile and olive filling, or cream cheese and finely chopped vegetable filling.

DRIED BEEF ROLL-UPS

1 3-ounce package cream cheese with chives
1-2 teaspoons milk
1 8-ounce package dried beef

In small mixing bowl, blend cream cheese and milk. Spread each piece of beef with cream cheese mixture and place in stacks of three. Roll each stack lengthwise. Wrap in plastic wrap and refrigerate until ready to serve. Then slice, spear with wooden pick and arrange on serving platter. Serves 8-10.

Per Serving: 75 calories; 4.3 fat grams

Before rolling, place long, thin slice of dill pickle on last piece of beef and cheese.

CORNED BEEF RIBBONS

A showy display of an ordinary sandwich.

12 thin slices white or whole wheat bread
1/4 cup butter or margarine, softened
1 1/2 cups cooked corned beef, ground
3 tablespoons dill pickle, finely chopped
3 tablespoons cream cheese at room
    temperature

Trim crusts from bread. Spread with butter. In small bowl, combine corned beef with pickle and cream cheese. Spread 8 slices of bread with corned beef mixture. Make 4 stacks of two each of the spread slices. Top with remaining slices. Wrap in plastic, label and freeze. To serve, defrost, cut each stack into 3 slices and cut slices in half. Serves 10-12.

Per Serving: 187 calories; 11.2 fat grams

 Chicken, beef or tuna can be substituted for corned beef. Use mayonnaise instead of butter.

HERB BEEF SAUSAGE

Make your own beef roll to give as gifts or to serve with cheese and crackers.

4 pounds lean ground beef
1/2 cup curing/pickling salt
3 tablespoons dry red wine
1 teaspoon garlic powder
2 tablespoons mustard seed
1 tablespoon basil
1 tablespoon oregano
1 teaspoon onion powder
2/3 cup parmesan cheese

In large bowl, mix all ingredients well. Form into 3-4 firm rolls. Wrap in foil with the shiny side against the rolls. Refrigerate 24 hours. Preheat oven to 325°. Punch holes in foil sides and bottom of rolls. Place on rack on baking pan and bake 1 1/2 hours. Unwrap and cool. Rewrap in plastic and foil. Refrigerate. Slice to serve. Each roll serves 8-10.

Per Serving: 174 calories; 13.3 fat grams

 This recipe goes together QUICKly but needs a little advanced planning.

HAM CUBES

These are just a little bit of work but add variety to the party table. Canape cutters make QUICK work with this 'sandwich'.

1 tablespoon horseradish
1 tablespoon mayonnaise
1 teaspoon Worcestershire sauce
1 teaspoon seasoned salt
1/8 teaspoon pepper
1 8-ounce package cream cheese at room
    temperature
6 thin slices boiled ham

In small bowl, beat all ingredients except ham together until creamy. Place 1 ham slice on waxed paper and spread small amount of cream cheese mixture on it. Place another slice of ham on top and repeat ending with ham slice. Wrap securely in waxed paper and place in freezer for 2 or more hours. About an hour before time to serve, remove from freezer and cut lengthwise then crosswise into small cubes. Pierce each cube with colored toothpick. Place on dish or stick in hors d'oeuvre fruit like pineapple. Serves 16.

Per Serving: 71 calories; 6.2 fat grams

 Add sliced cheese between ham and cream cheese mixture.

HAM AND CHEESE PINWHEELS

These little tidbits are great served with fruit as a kabob.

1 8-ounce package light cream cheese at
    room temperature
1 tablespoon spicy mustard
1 tablespoon chives, chopped
10 slices thinly sliced ham
10 slices cheese

In small mixer bowl, beat cream cheese until smooth; stir in mustard and chives. Spread each meat slice with about 1 tablespoon cheese mixture; top with cheese slice and spread with another table-spoon cheese mixture. Roll up. Chill. Before serving, slice each roll into 5 pieces. Serves 25.

Per Serving: 207 calories; 16.4 fat grams

 Summer sausage or pepper loaf can be used in place of ham for a unique taste.

DILLED SHRIMP

Early preparation leads to ease in serving.

1 1/2 cups light mayonnaise
1/3 cup lemon juice
1/4 cup sugar
1/2 cup light sour cream
1 large red onion, thinly sliced
2 tablespoons dill
1/4 teaspoon salt
2 pounds cooked medium shrimp

In large bowl, mix all ingredients, except shrimp, together. Stir in shrimp. Cover and refrigerate overnight. Stir once. Serve with wooden picks. Serves 8-10.

Per serving: 182 calories; 4.1 fat grams

SHRIMP COCKTAIL

This recipe calls for individual shrimp cocktail glasses, but it can be served in a large decorative bowl.

6 lettuce leaves
2 cups shredded lettuce
3/4 pound cooked shrimp
Shrimp cocktail sauce
1 lemon, cut in wedges

Cocktail Sauce:

1/2-1 cup catsup
2 tablespoons horseradish
1 tablespoon grated onion
2 tablespoons lemon juice
1 teaspoon garlic salt
1 teaspoon Worcestershire sauce
Dash pepper

Place lettuce leaf in each cocktail glass and top with 1/3 cup shredded lettuce. Place shrimp around edge of glass. In small bowl, combine all cocktail sauce ingredients and chill. Pour in center right onto lettuce or in a small dish (small baking/party cups work well). Serves 6.

Per Serving: 45 calories; 0.3 fat grams

Try shrimp with guacamole served in half an avocado shell placed on a bed of lettuce.

Cold Hors d'oeuvres

Notes:

Hot Hors d'oeuvres

CHEESE SURPRISES

The surprise is what's hidden in the center of each piece.

2 cups cheddar cheese, grated
1/2 cup butter, softened
1 cup flour
1/2 teaspoon hot sauce
1/2 teaspoon salt
1/2 teaspoon paprika
24 medium green olives
24 pieces water chestnuts
24 pieces pepperoni

Preheat oven to 400°. Blend cheese and butter. Add remaining ingredients. Wrap 1 teaspoon cheese mixture around each green olive, water chestnut and pepperoni piece. Bake 15 minutes. Serve warm. Makes about 72. Serves 24.

Per serving: 140 calories; 9.9 fat grams

CHILE CHEESE PUFFS

9 slices white sandwich bread
1 cup sharp cheddar cheese, shredded
1/2 cup butter or margarine, softened
1 4-ounce can chopped green chiles
1/2 teaspoon chili powder

Preheat oven to 400°. Trim crusts from bread; cut into fourths. Place on sprayed baking sheet. In medium bowl, blend remaining ingredients. Place heaping teaspoonful of mixture on each bread square. Bake 10 minutes, or until puffy and lightly browned. Serves 18.

Per serving: 105 calories; 7.6 fat grams

Foot Notes

Vary by adding 1-2 chopped green onions and dash of hot pepper sauce to cheese mixture.

Vary by replacing green chilies with 1/2 cup finely chopped fresh mushrooms and adding 3 tablespoons parmesan cheese.

ELEGANT CREAMY PIE

An attractive, savory hors d'oeuvre that is decorated in fresh vegetables. Prepare ahead and QUICKly add vegetables at last minute.

1 9-inch frozen pastry shell, thawed
1 12-ounce container cream cheese
2-ounces blue cheese, optional (use shred-
    ded white cheddar cheese, instead)
1/2 cup light mayonnaise
1/2 teaspoon onion or garlic salt
8 cherry tomatoes, halved,
8 fresh mushrooms, sliced
1/2 cup fresh parsley, chopped,
2 hard boiled eggs, chopped
1/4 cup ripe olives, sliced

Preheat oven to 400°. On large baking sheet, pat pastry into 11-inch circle. Pierce with fork. Bake 8 minutes. Cool. Place carefully on serving platter. In large bowl, beat remaining ingredients until fluffy. Spread on pastry and cover. Chill until ready to serve. Garnish with vegetables, starting on the outside with tomato halves sliced part down. Then lay mushrooms down, overlapping at stems. Lay parsley sprigs in center and sprinkle egg and olives over open area. Cut into wedges. Serves 10-12.

Per serving: 254 calories; 18.9 fat grams

 Foot Note For QUICK topping, chop vegetables, except tomatoes, and toss together. Spoon over top of pie. Garnish with tomatoes.

TRADITIONAL STUFFED MUSHROOMS

Cooks have their own 'traditional' stuffed mushrooms; this is ours.

1 pound medium mushrooms
1/4 cup green pepper, finely chopped
1/4 cup onion, finely chopped
1/4 cup butter or margarine
1 1/2 cups soft bread crumbs (3-4 slices)
1/4 cup Monterey Jack cheese, shredded
1/2 teaspoon salt
1/2 teaspoon thyme
1/4 teaspoon turmeric
1/4 teaspoon white pepper

Preheat oven to 300°. Remove stems from mushrooms and chop. In small skillet, saute stems, green pepper and onion in butter 2-3 minutes. Add remaining ingredients and toss. Remove from heat. Fill mushroom caps with mixture. Place on baking sheet and bake 15 minutes. Serve immediately. Serves 8-10.

Per serving: 133 calories; 7.2 fat grams

SPINACH-FILLED MUSHROOMS

2 pounds large mushrooms
1 cup onion, finely chopped
3 tablespoons butter or margarine
1 10-ounce package frozen spinach, drained
    and finely chopped
1/2 cup Swiss cheese, grated
Parmesan cheese

Preheat oven to 300°. Remove stems from mush-rooms and chop. In fry pan, saute stems and onion in butter 2-3 minutes. Add spinach, stirring to mix. Cook 5 minutes. Add Swiss cheese and toss lightly. Remove from heat and fill mushroom caps with mixture. Sprinkle with parmesan cheese. Place in sprayed, shallow baking pan. Bake 15 minutes. Serve immediately. Serves 8-10.

Per serving: 101 calories; 6.4 fat grams

For really QUICK and unusual stuffed spinach mushrooms, defrost 1 12-ounce package frozen spinach souffle, fill mushrooms caps and sprinkle with parmesan cheese. Bake 15 minutes at 300°.

HOT MUSHROOM CANAPES

Georgie's friend, Babette, created this delicious stuffed mushroom canape.

1 pound mushrooms, washed, drained and
    chopped
1/4 cup butter
1 cup onion, finely chopped
1/3 cup flour
1/3 cup milk
1/2 teaspoon salt
1/8 teaspoon pepper
1 loaf sliced white bread
Parmesan cheese

Turn oven to broil. In small skillet, saute mushrooms and onions in butter 5 minutes until liquid has evaporated. Add flour gradually. Mix well. Gradually stir in milk. Add salt and pepper. Continue cooking until thickened. Cool. Cut bread into rounds with biscuit cutter. Spread each with 1 tablespoon mushroom mixture. Sprinkle with parmesan cheese. Broil 5 minutes to brown. Serves 8-10.

Per serving: 244 calories; 8.3 fat grams

POTATO SKINS

Rarely do we deep fry foods, but these normally deep fried favorites are just as welcomed when baked.

4 large baking potatoes, baked
3 tablespoons olive oil
1 tablespoon parmesan cheese
1 1/2 teaspoons seasoned salt
1/8 teaspoon pepper
8 bacon strips, cooked and crumbled
1 1/2 cups cheddar cheese, shredded
1/2 cup sour cream
4 green onions, chopped

Preheat oven to 450°. Cut potatoes in half lengthwise; scoop out pulp, leaving a 1/4 inch shell. Reserve pulp for another use. Place potatoes on sprayed baking sheet. In small bowl, combine oil, parmesan cheese, salt and pepper. Brush both sides of skins and bake 7 minutes; turn with tongs. Bake 7 more minutes until crispy around edges. Sprinkle bacon and cheese evenly inside skins. Return to oven 2 minutes longer until cheese is melted. Top with sour cream and onions. Serve immediately. Serves 8.

Per serving: 242 calories; 18.5 fat grams

 Freeze reserved potato pulp for use in soups or casseroles at a later time.

BACON-CHEESE BOARDS

Prepare this early in the day and freeze until ready to bake.

2 cups cheddar cheese, shredded
1 6-ounce can black olives, chopped
1 cup light mayonnaise
2 tablespoons onion, chopped
6 slices bacon, cooked crisp and crumbled
1 package cocktail rye bread
1 cup mozzarella cheese, shredded

In large bowl, mix cheddar cheese, olives, mayonnaise, onion and bacon together. Arrange bread on sprayed baking sheets. Spread mixture on bread. Top each slice with 1 teaspoon mozzarella cheese. Freeze until ready to bake. Heat oven to 350°. Bake 15 minutes. Remove to serving platter. Serves 20-24.

Per serving: 108 calories; 7.2 fat grams

Whole wheat cocktail bread is also available.

Serve these as a stand alone appetizer or as an accompaniment to a fruit salad or soup.

BACON-WATER CHESTNUTS

Prepare these popular treats ahead of time and refrigerate until ready to broil.

2 8-ounce cans water chestnuts
1/2 cup Worcestershire sauce or soy sauce
2 tablespoons sugar
1 pound lean bacon strips, cut in half

Preheat broiler of oven. Drain water chestnuts and cut very large ones in half. Leave drained chestnuts in can and cover with soy sauce. Let stand 10 minutes, then drain. Sprinkle with sugar. Wrap bacon strip around each water chestnut and secure with toothpick. Place under broiler 4-5 minutes until bacon is crisp. Serve immediately. Serves 8-10.

Per serving: 337 calories; 24.9 fat grams

Same idea with black olives: drain 1 6-ounce can medium pitted ripe olives. Stuff cavities of olives with 1/2 cup finely minced onion. Cut bacon in half lengthwise, then crosswise into fourths. Wrap each olive with bacon. Place in shallow baking pan or broiler pan. Broil 4-5 minutes. Drain on paper towels.

HAM AND CHEESE MINIS

Besides being the hit of a party, these little sandwiches can be frozen for a quick lunch or snack.

24 small sandwich buns (usually a special
    order in bakery department)
24 slices deli ham
24 slices Swiss cheese

Topping:

1/2 cup margarine
1 1/2 tablespoons poppy seed
1 teaspoon Worcestershire Sauce
1 tablespoon onion flakes
1 tablespoon mustard (spicy if preferred)

Preheat oven to 350°. Make buns, ham and cheese into 24 small sandwiches placing each on a heavy piece of foil. Combine topping ingredients and pour over sandwiches. Wrap foil around each sandwich. Bake 10-12 minutes. Makes 24.

Per serving: 246 calories; 13.9 fat grams

 Great for camping; just throw on the campfire coals to heat.

Hot Hors d'oeuvres

HAM PUFFS

Very easy and tasty morsels.

1 10-ounce package crescent roll dough
1 egg
1/4 pound shaved ham, chopped
1 1/2 tablespoons onion, minced
1 clove garlic, minced
1 tablespoon green pepper, minced
1/2 cup Monterey Jack cheese, shredded

Preheat oven to 350°. On cutting board, unroll, mend seams and cut into 14 2-inch squares. Place in sprayed mini muffin pans. In small bowl, beat egg. Add all other ingredients and mix well. Drop about a teaspoonful into each cup. Bake 15 minutes. Serves 6-8.

Per serving: 190 calories; 9.3 fat grams

PIGS IN THE BLANKET

Cyndi remembers having these as a child, but with regular sized hot dogs.

1 16-ounce package cocktail wieners or
    smoked cocktail wieners
3/4 cup soy sauce
1 can crescent roll dough or biscuit dough

Preheat oven to 400°. In large bowl, marinate wieners in soy sauce for 1 hour. Separate rolls and cut each into 2 wedges. Wrap around wieners starting with large end. Place on large baking sheet and bake 10 minutes. Serve hot. Serves 10-12.

Per serving: 107 calories; 5.8 fat grams

These little wieners are good mixed with barbecue sauce in a slow cooker. Heat for 2-3 hours while preparing other hors d'oeuvres.

ITALIAN SAUSAGE PIZZA TIDBITS

Partially bake the crust but wait to spread remaining ingredients until just before serving time. Then bake, cut, remove to serving platter and keep warm on warming tray.

2 8-ounce cans refrigerated crescent rolls
3/4 pound Italian sausage
1 onion, chopped
1-2 cloves garlic, minced
1 15-ounce can crushed plum tomatoes
1/4 cup Parmesan cheese
1 teaspoon basil, fresh or dried
1/2 teaspoon thyme
1 teaspoon oregano
1 teaspoon parsley
3/4 cup Monterey Jack cheese, shredded
3/4 cup Mozzarella cheese, shredded

Preheat oven to 450°. Spray baking pan lightly with non-stick spray. Separate and spread crescent roll dough onto 15x10x1-inch baking pan. Bake 5 minutes. In large frying pan, brown sausage; drain well. Add onion and garlic. Simmer 5 minutes. Add tomatoes, parmesan cheese, basil, thyme, oregano and parsley. Simmer 5 minutes. Spread over crust. Sprinkle with cheeses and bake 10-12 minutes. Remove and cut into 50-60 appetizer-sized pieces. Serve immediately.

Per serving: 46 calories; 2.6 fat grams

 Foot Note To vary, spread red and green pepper slices, mushrooms, black or green olives, or any other vegetable of choice on top before baking.

SAUSAGE BALLS

Very simple to prepare; gone in a flash.

1 pound sausage
1 pound cheddar cheese, grated
3 cups biscuit mix

Preheat oven to 300°. In large bowl, mix all ingredients together. Shape into 1-inch balls and place on sprayed baking sheet. Bake 20 minutes until lightly browned. Serves 20-30.

Per serving: 139 calories; 8.7 fat grams

 Crumble any leftovers to make crust for an egg casserole.

Hot Hors d'oeuvres

SAUSAGE POTATO SQUARES

1/2 pound sausage
1 cup frozen hash brown potatoes, shredded
1 8-ounce package processed cheese
1 package party rye bread

In medium skillet, brown sausage; drain. Add potatoes and cheese; stir until melted. Place bread on sprayed baking sheet. Spread sausage mixture on top of bread. Freeze. Broil 5 minutes. Remove to serving tray. Serves 15.

Per serving: 150 calories; 8.2 fat grams

Omit the potatoes and make a dip out of the sausage and cheese. If necessary, add milk to thin. Keep warm in slow cooker and serve as a dip with rye bread.

For holiday treats, cut out thin sliced bread with cookie cutters. Substitute bacon, ground beef, turkey or chicken for the sausage.

SWEET AND SOUR MEATBALLS

This dish can be prepared early in the day and simmered in a slow cooker. Very quick and easy to serve.

1 pound lean ground beef
1 1/2 teaspoons salt
1/4 teaspoon pepper
1 8-ounce can water chestnuts, drained and
    chopped
2 tablespoons oil
2 tablespoons cornstarch
1/2 cup sugar
1/2 cup vinegar
1 tablespoon soy sauce
1 green pepper, cut in large chunks
1 8-ounce can pineapple chunks with juice

Combine ground beef, salt, pepper and water chestnuts. Shape into 3/4-inch meatballs. In large skillet, heat oil and brown meatballs. In large saucepan, combine remaining ingredients. Bring to boil; reduce heat. Add meatballs. Simmer 5 minutes. Serves 8.

Per serving: 28l calories; 15.2 fat grams

Use bottled sweet and sour sauce; add pineapple, green pepper, watter chestnuts and cooked meatballs. Georgie buys frozen precooked meatballs that she heats in the microwave, drains and adds them to any number of recipes. Less than half the work and she still gets great compliments.

Hot Hors d'oeuvres

MILD MEXICAN MEATBALLS

Meatballs with a south of the border flair.

1 1/2 pounds lean ground beef
1 large egg
3/4 cup bread crumbs
1/2 teaspoon ground black pepper
1 1/4 teaspoons salt
3 cloves garlic, minced
1/4 cup water
2 teaspoons oil
1 small onion, finely chopped
1 teaspoon cumin
1 28-ounce can crushed tomatoes
1 poblano chile pepper or 1 8-ounce can
    diced green chiles
1 cup chicken broth
1/4 cup cilantro, coarsely chopped

In large bowl, mix beef, egg, bread crumbs, pepper, 1 teaspoon salt, 1 garlic clove and water. Shape into 3/4-inch meatballs and place in large pan with oil. Add onion, cumin, 2 cloves garlic and 1/4 teaspoon salt. Cook 5 minutes, gently lifting and turning meatballs until browned. Stir in tomatoes, chile and chicken broth. Stir gently. Heat to boiling; lower heat and simmer uncovered 15 minutes. Spoon into chafing dish and garnish with cilantro. Serve with cocktail picks. Serves 20.

Per serving: 131 calories; 8.3 fat grams

Foot Note Meatballs can be made ahead of event and frozen. Keep on hand for a quick addition to pasta sauce.

TAMALE BITES

Like other meatballs, these can be made ahead and frozen. Bake as needed or simmer in slow cooker.

2 cups corn bread, crumbled
1 10-ounce can mild enchilada sauce
1/2 teaspoon salt
1 1/2 pounds lean ground beef
1 8-ounce can tomato sauce
1/2 cup Monterey Jack cheese, shredded

In large bowl, combine corn bread crumbs, 1/2 can enchilada sauce and salt. Add ground beef and mix well. Shape into 1-inch balls. Place in shallow baking pan. Bake, uncovered 18-20 minutes or until done. Meanwhile, in small sauce pan, heat remaining enchilada sauce and tomato sauce. Place meatballs in chafing dish and pour sauce over all. Top with cheese. Serve with wooden picks. Serves 20-30.

Per serving: 156 calories; 9.5 fat grams

 Freeze leftover corn bread to use for another recipe.

Hot Hors d'oeuvres

SALSA BITS

These can be served hot or cold. They are super either way.

1 8-ounce container cream cheese at room
    temperature
1/3 cup thick and chunky salsa
2 eggs
1/2 cup cheddar cheese, shredded
2 tablespoons black olives, chopped
1 tablespoon green onion, chopped
1 clove garlic, minced
1/4 cup sour cream
2 tablespoons fresh cilantro, chopped

Preheat oven to 350°. Spray muffin cups. Whisk cream cheese, salsa and eggs together. Stir in remaining ingredients, except sour cream and cilantro. Fill muffin cups 3/4 full. Bake 15 minutes or until center is set. Cool in pan 5 minutes and remove to serving tray or cooling rack. Spread tops with small amount of sour cream and garnish with cilantro. Serves 24.

Per serving: 56 calories; 5.2 fat grams

STUFFED POPPERS

With the cheesy stuffing, these jalapeño poppers are a tasty mouthful.

1 pound fresh jalapeños, halved lengthwise
    and seeded
1 8-ounce package cream cheese, softened
1 cup sharp cheddar cheese, shredded
1 cup Monterey Jack cheese, shredded
3 bacon strips, cooked and crumbled
1/3 cup red bell pepper, minced
2 green onions, chopped
1/4 teaspoon chili powder
1/2 teaspoon garlic salt
1/2 cup dried bread crumbs

Preheat oven to 300°. Place jalapeño halves on sprayed baking pan. In large bowl, combine cheeses, bacon, pepper, green onions and seasonings. Spoon about 2 tablespoons into each pepper half. Sprinkle with bread crumbs. Bake 30 minutes. Serve with sour cream on the side. Serves 10-12.

Per serving: 197 calories; 15.0 fat grams

When working with any kind of hot peppers, use rubber or plastic gloves to protect your hands.

Shorter baking time will produce spicier flavor; longer baking time will produce milder taste.

STACKED QUESADILLAS

These can be cut into hors d' oeuvres sizes or served as individual 'pizzas' for lunch or dinner.

1 4-ounce can diced green chiles
2 cups Monterey jack cheese, shredded
1/2 cup frozen corn
2 green onions, chopped
6 fajita-size flour tortillas
Salsa
Cilantro

In medium bowl, combine all ingredients, except tortillas. Spray medium skillet. Place 1 tortilla in pan over medium-high heat. Spread 1/3 chile mixture over tortilla and top with another one. Cook 1-2 minutes on each side until golden brown. Repeat 2 times using remaining ingredients. Serve with salsa and cilantro. Cut each into 4 wedges. Serves 12.

Per serving: 138 calories; 7.0 fat grams

A pizza cutter works great to slice these quesadillas.

Sausage, ground beef, shredded chicken or beef can be added to these for a heartier hors d'oeuvre. For QUICKer heating, use microwave to heat. They will be soft and just as good.

BLACK BEAN AND SPINACH QUESADILLAS

Don't be scared by the list of ingredients. This recipe isn't nearly as difficult as it appears.

1 1/2 teaspoons olive oil
2 tablespoons onion, finely chopped
2 tablespoons jalapeño pepper, seeded and
    finely chopped
1 teaspoon minced garlic
6-8 cherry tomatoes, quartered
1 14-ounce can black beans
1 cup fresh or frozen corn, optional
1/4 teaspoon cayenne pepper
1/2 teaspoon oregano
1/2 teaspoon cumin
6 fajita-size flour tortillas
1 1/2-2 cups fresh baby spinach leaves,
    washed and drained
1/2 cup sharp cheddar cheese, grated

In large nonstick skillet, saute onion, jalapeño, garlic and tomatoes in olive oil about 2 minutes until onion is soft. Add black beans with liquid and corn. Stir in cayenne, oregano and cumin. Cook about 5 minutes until most of the liquid is evaporated. Spray and heat griddle or large skillet. Place tortilla in skillet and top with 1/3 bean mixture, 1/3 spinach and 1/3 cheese. Top with second tortilla. Cook over medium-high heat about 1 minute until lightly browned. Carefully turn to brown other side. Remove to serving platter and cut into wedges. Repeat with other tortillas, beans, spinach and cheese. Serve with fresh salsa. Serves 12.

Per serving: 160 calories; 4.0 fat grams

Foot Note For QUICK chicken quesadillas, heat chicken in salsa. Spread tortilla with refried beans, layer of chicken mixture and top with shredded cheddar cheese. Bake 15 minutes at 400°.

MEXICAN SANDWICH

Cut into larger pieces and serve for lunch with tortilla chips and a garden salad.

3 large flour tortillas
1 8-ounce can spicy bean dip
2 tablespoons sour cream
2 tablespoons salsa
1/2 teaspoon garlic salt
1/2 teaspoon cumin
1/2 teaspoon chili powder
1/4 teaspoon oregano
2 cups chicken, cooked and chopped, or 2
    10-ounce cans cooked chicken,
    separated into small pieces
1/2 cup cilantro, chopped
1 red pepper, chopped
8-10 green onions, chopped
1 15-ounce can black olives, sliced
2 cups white cheddar cheese, shredded
1 tomato, chopped

Preheat oven to 400°. Spray large round casserole dish (pottery makes nice serving appearance). Place one tortilla on bottom. In medium mixing bowl, combine bean dip, sour cream, salsa, garlic salt, cumin, chili powder and oregano; spread on tortilla. Cover with second tortilla. Layer chicken, cilantro, pepper, onion, olives and 1 cup cheese on top. Cover with third tortilla and top with remaining cheese. Bake 10-12 minutes. Garnish with tomato. Cut into 8-10 pie-shaped pieces. Serve hot.

Per serving: 341 calories; 16.6 fat grams

TASTY CHICKEN WINGS

This is a great recipe to prepare in the slow cooker.

1 8-ounce bottle barbecue sauce
1/2 cup catsup
1/4 cup soy sauce
1 teaspoon hot pepper flakes
2-3 drops hot pepper sauce
1 64-ounce package frozen chicken wings,
    thawed if you want to cut into
    three pieces

Place all ingredients, except chicken wings, in slow cooker. Stir until mixed well. Add chicken wings stirring to cover with sauce. Cover and cook on low 6-8 hours. Remove to platter and spoon on extra sauce. Serves 12.

Per serving: 208 calories; 13.4 fat grams

For a sweeter, teriyaki flavor, add 1/4 cup honey or 1/8 cup honey and 1/8 cup molasses.

Make really quick sauce for wings using equal parts catsup and coke.

CRAB AND SHRIMP ON ENGLISH MUFFINS

A great seafood combination in hors d'oeuvres, salads, enchiladas or burritos

1/2 cup butter
1/2 cup sharp cheddar cheese, shredded
1 6-ounce can crab meat
1 7-ounce can small shrimp, chopped;
    reserve 32 shrimp for garnish
1 tablespoon onion, finely grated
1 teaspoon lemon juice
8 English muffins
Cayenne pepper to taste
Paprika to taste

Set oven on broil. Cream butter and cheese. Add crabmeat, shrimp, onion and lemon juice. Mix. Spread mixture on muffins. Sprinkle each with cayenne pepper and paprika. Broil 3-4 minutes until lightly browned. Remove and quickly quarter each muffin. Cut into squares. Garnish with reserved shrimp. Serves 12-16.

Per serving: 180 calories; 8.9 fat grams

 A QUICKer option: roll crescent roll dough onto baking stone or 9x13-inch baking sheet. Spread crab mixture over dough. Bake 5-7 minutes at 400°. Garnish with reserved shrimp.

SALMON STUFFED ROLLS

1 8-ounce can smoked salmon, drained
1 teaspoon horseradish
2 tablespoons light mayonnaise
2 tablespoons lemon juice
1 teaspoon onion, grated
2 ready-made pie crusts
Paprika

Preheat oven to 425°. In large bowl, mix salmon, horseradish, mayonnaise, lemon juice and onion together. Place 1 pie crust on cutting board and spread with salmon mixture. Cut into 16 wedges. Roll up from round edge. Fork holes into top of each roll and sprinkle with paprika. Place on baking sheet. Repeat with remaining pie crust. Bake 15 minutes. Serve immediately. Serves 16.

Per serving: 119 calories; 6.8 fat grams

 Seasoned mustard or dill weed can be substituted for horseradish.

POTATO QUICHE BASKETS

These little 'baskets' are so cute on an hors d'oeuvre table or breakfast buffet.

1/2 cup butter, melted
1 10-ounce package frozen hash browns, thawed
1/2 cup onions, finely chopped
1/2 cup green pepper, finely chopped
2 slices ham, thinly sliced
4 eggs
3 tablespoons milk
1/2 teaspoon pepper
1/2 teaspoon salt

In 3 mini muffin tins, brush butter around cups. With fingers, press 1 tablespoon hash browns into cup making a basket. In small skillet, saute onions, green pepper and ham 5 minutes. Set aside. In small bowl, beat eggs with milk, pepper and salt. Add sauteed onion mixture and stir. Fill each muffin cup 3/4 full. Bake 15-20 minutes until eggs are puffed and slightly browned. Serves 6-8.

Per serving: 260 calories; 21.9 fat grams

 Try substituting sausage for the ham, using favorite combination of vegetables or spicing up quiche baskets with herbs.

CHEESY WONTON CUPS

Cyndi substitutes zucchini for the artichokes, when it is in season, and adds onion.

24 small wonton wrappers
2 6-ounce jars marinated artichoke hearts,
    drained, reserving marinade, and
    chopped
1/4 cup red pepper, chopped
1/3 cup black olives, sliced
1/4 cup parmesan cheese
1 clove garlic, minced
1/2 cup mayonnaise

Preheat oven to 350°. Spray muffin tins. Press wonton wrappers into muffin cups. In large bowl, combine remaining ingredients and mix. Spoon artichoke mixture into muffin cups. Bake 12-14 minutes. Remove and let stand 2 minutes. Carefully transfer to serving tray. Serves 24.

Per serving: 70 calories; 4.2 fat grams

To loosen peel from garlic clove, press firmly into counter with heel of hand.

Notes:

Index

Cold Hors d'oeuvres

Hot Hors d'oeuvres